Leadership Through Values

A Study in Personal and Organizational Development

Brian P. Hall
and Helen Thompson
Consultant Author: William Zierdt

Paulist Press
New York, Ramsey, Toronto

**this book is dedicated to
George Boyle
for his continuing support
in the Omega Project**

DESIGN:
Gloria Ortíz

PHOTO CREDITS:
Robert Mullin, p. 5
Robert Beckhard, p. 11
Paul M. Schrock, pp. 13, 26, 38, 45, 60, 82, 97, 98
Vivienne della Grotta, pp. 17, 72
John Glaser, p. 32
Tom McCarthy, pp. 53, 67

Library of Congress
Catalog Card Number: 80-81438

ISBN: 0-8091-2313-4
Published by Paulist Press
545 Island Road, Ramsey, N.J. 07446

Printed and bound in the
United States of America

Contents

Prologue 11
CHAPTER I:
Leadership Theory and Skill Development 13
FUTURE REALITIES 13
LEADERSHIP THEORY: A HISTORICAL SURVEY 15
    Efficiency and Productivity: Developing Instrumental Skills
    Humanistic Two-Dimensional Theories: Developing
    Interpersonal Skills
    Leadership as "Origination"; Skills of the Imagination
    The Situation Surrounding a Leader: Envisioning the System
    Summary
FOUR KINDS OF SKILLS 29
CONCLUSION 31

CHAPTER II:
A Theory of Consciousness and Value Development 32
THE PHASES OF CONSCIOUSNESS AND VALUE DEVELOPMENT 33
    Phase One Consciousness
    Phase Two Consciousness
    The Transition to Phase Three
    Phase Three Consciousness
    Phase Four Consciousness
    The Four Phases: A Summary
THE STAGES OF VALUE DEVELOPMENT 47
    Values and Meaning
    Shifts in Consciousness
    Values and Skill Development

CHAPTER III:
Toward Servant Leadership 53
SEVEN LEADERSHIP FOLLOWERSHIP STYLES 54
    Level 1: The Alienated Man
    Level 2: The Preservative Man
    Level 3: The Organization Man
    Level 4: The Communal Man
    Level 5: The Independent Man
    Level 6: The Creator Man
    Level 7: Man as Prophet
    Leadership/Followership Styles: A Summary
DEVELOPING LEADERSHIP:
CONSCIOUSNESS AND VALUE THEORY REVISITED 63
The Leader as Autocrat: Levels 1, 2, and 3
    Autocratic Leadership: A Summary
Laissez-faire Leadership Style: Level 4
    Imagination and Interpersonal Skills
    Professional Peer Support
    Laissez-faire Leadership: A Summary

63473

Toward Servant Leadership: Levels 5 and 6
    The Genesis of Systems Skills
    Systems Skills: The Bridge to Level 6
    Servant Leadership Summarized

CHAPTER IV:
Motivation: Why Some Persons Lead
and Others, Who Could, Do Not 82
TOWARD A THEORY OF MOTIVATION 83
    Integrated Skill Development
    Support Groupings
    Opportunity Within the Organization
TWO CASE STUDIES 90
    The Case of Joe
    The Case of Mr. Patel
SOME FINAL OBSERVATIONS 95

V. EPILOGUE:
Leadership Theory Revisited 98
    Leadership Levels and Administrative Theory and Research
    An Effort to Build On but Go Beyond
APPENDIX A: 104
Ends Values in their Stage of Development—Means Values in their Stage
of Development
APPENDIX B: 106
Values as Skills
APPENDIX C: 108
The Interrelationships: Four Phases of Consciousness —Eight Stages of
Value Development—Seven Levels of Leadership
BIBLIOGRAPHY 110

Preface

The purpose of this Preface is to explain to the reader the process whereby the present work came about, so as to give appropriate credit to those persons whose work resulted in its development. The book is the consequence of thirteen years of research by Brian Hall in consultation with a number of people at various points in that time period.

Co-author Dr. Helen Thompson took a year to intern with the Center for the Exploration of Values and Meaning (CEVAM) in 1977 after completing her term as dean of Clark College in Iowa. It was she who wrote this book in consultation with Brian Hall, constructing all the relevant research, data, and information from Hall's theory of values. Though she was not involved in the research of the theory itself, she was involved closely with Brian Hall in its final stages for approximately three years. In the actual writing of the book, Hall met regularly with Helen Thompson in the development of all the major reconstructions, diagrams and so forth. It is therefore with great indebtedness that we thank her for a final manuscript. At the same time, we want to be clear

about all the other contributions to the research and development over the years.

The research began initially in 1965, when Hall spent time with Ivan Illich, Paulo Freire, and Eric Fromm in Cuernavaca, Mexico. The influence there was particularly to note how unwittingly foreign personnel impose values on other cultures, often creating social and management conflicts destructive to the indigenous culture. After completing a doctor's degree, studying psychoanalysis and traditional healing in the churches, Hall worked in the Gary community in northern Indiana for a number of years with Micheal Kenney, now a management consultant in Indianapolis with volunteer organizations.

It was Kenney at the outset who enabled Hall to put his own experience of psychoanalysis into a value perspective. Hall then developed a specific theory of values that related to personal development that was published in three books, called **Value Clarification as Learning Process** (Paulist Press, 1973).

Many of the growth exercises in the second volume were developed by Hall and Kenney. The purpose of this book, initially, was to explore the value issue in more depth, since at that time much had been written by other authors of a more or less superficial nature on value clarification in the public schools. The purpose was to try to see values as formative to people's lives.

At that point, Paulist Press, under the leadership of its President, Kevin Lynch, and its Editor (at that time), Richard Payne, encouraged the use of this material to be researched and developed as curriculum for public education. The point was that the value approach should have a developmental effect in terms of holistic health for individuals outside of the counseling situation. Paulist Press put a great deal of money, effort and personal support into this values venture with the result that CEVAM was created. Bishop John Craine of Indianapolis, and Richard Kunkel, now Chairman of the Department of Education at the University of Nevada, Las Vegas, were prime movers in its design and development.

CEVAM, which was later called the Center for Values and Management, was then aided in its research by a considerable grant from the Lilly Endowment. Particular thanks go to Earle McGraith and Charles Williams of the Endowment for the initial encouragement of the project.

From 1973 until late 1976 CEVAM, with the help of its new Vice President, Dr. Eileen Cantin, and Mr. Patrick Smith, Hall enlarged on the theory of value development. Once the curriculum had begun for Paulist Press, a number of research consultants were brought in from Canada and the United States. In particular, we would mention Dr. Anne Colby of the Lawrence Kohlberg team, and Dr. Julius Elias, presently Dean of Arts and Sciences at Stalls University in Connecticut. "Project Values" was then put into action and dealt not only with education as curriculum in the public schools, but with the development of administration in a number of small colleges through a project-values venture called the "Mandala Project." All the research for this project and its evaluation components were carried out by Dr. Richard Kunkel to whom we are especially grateful. His own value approach to the program was published at St. Louis University in 1976 in an article called "Overview of Program Evaluation Literature: An Introduction to the Perception-Based Theory of Program Evaluation." This was written in conjunction with Dr. Susan A. Tucker. Dr. Kunkel was, at that time, Head of the Department of Education at St. Louis University, which shared "Project Values" as a joint project with CEVAM.

The consequence of the research and development was the publication by Brian Hall of **Development of Consciousness: A Confluent Theory of Values** (Paulist Press, 1976). This first publication on the theory itself constitutes a large part of the first half of this book.

In 1975, CEVAM initiated a joint project with the Second Presbyterian Church, Indianapolis, also supported by the Lilly Endowment. Named the "Omega Project," the purpose was twofold: (1) to test out the theory with management and leadership both in the USA and in international circles, and (2) to do so in a church setting to learn whether the theory would be as effective there in a quasi-therapeutic mode as in the public-education setting being experienced through "Project Values." Dr. George Boyle, whose contribution has been invaluable, joined Dr. Hall in the supervision of this project. The program was designed to examine the therapeutic aspects of the theory by diagnosing a person's levels of value development and then applying traditional methods of psychotherapy and some of the other traditional methods of relaxation, meditation, and bio-feeback.

The second aspect of this program was to get back into the international arena and to look at the question of value-based management leadership across cultural lines. Consequently, an international symposium on leadership management was held in Indianapolis in 1976 under the auspices of the "Omega Project." It was from this conference that new research data, on the stages of leadership development and the application of skill development, were initiated. The International Symposium, CEVAM, was supervised by the previous Director of the Indian Social Institute in New Delhi, Anthony D'Souza. Tony is now Rector of Xavier College, University of Bombay, and the Xavier Management Institute where CEVAM conducted programs on a regular basis. It was also at this leadership institute that Benjamin Tonna, who now directs the CEVAM Omega Center in Malta, also became interested in the theory and began to promote CEVAM leadership-development programs in Rome during 1977–78. Particular thanks are due both Anthony D'Souza and Benjamin Tonna for their contributions in the leadership-management area. Two articles were published in **Social Action,** New Delhi, in 1976, relating the need for leadership development in training as it related to the phases of consciousness. These articles were co-authored with Dr. Eileen Cantin and Patrick Smith whose five years of service with CEVAM were invaluable.

It was during this period that a special project was initiated in Seattle with the help of Mr. Gregory Barlow and Dr. William Sullivan. PSI-PRIVATE SECTOR INITIATIVE was a program designed to raise employment in Seattle in the private sector. This was an opportunity for CEVAM to test out the use of goal-setting methods with a complex organization that had many cross-cultural differences due to the complexity of the board members of that institution. They had failed over a one-year period to come to agreed-upon objectives and program. Using the value methods, this was accomplished in a relatively short period and moved a city-wide project forward considerably. This could not have happened without a certain amount of risk-taking on the part of Greg Barlow, to whom thanks are due here.

It is owing to this and other similar projects, particularly in India and Rome, that the confluent theory was completed with the stages of development, the skill section and the last chapter in this book on motivation. We give particular thanks to Patrick Smith who died suddenly in April of 1977 of a heart attack. His contribution in the area of imaginal skills was invaluable.

Finally, during these years, a considerable number of training and development workshops were done with the U.S. Army, Air Force, and Navy. Of particular assistance here was Colonel William Zierdt of the Leadership Training Division of the U.S. Army at Fort Benjamin Harrison in Indianapolis. By taking all the various aspects of research on leadership development since the 1900's, Bill was able to relate various cross-patterns of development to the value theory as well as point out where the holes were and the different aspects needing work. One aspect was motivation. This historical aspect of the research was included in this book to make it more viable as a general text, and was written by Bill and integrated into the earlier chapters.

Since 1976, a number of consultations have been carried out with corporations both within the U.S. and overseas. Regular training programs take place in our center in Malta for the Middle East and Europe, and in Bombay for Asia. Consequently, special programs related to executive development, sales and personnel development, and particularly systems analysis for corporations have been conducted. The emphasis is to try to train as many executives with personnel within corporations to do their own value-based analysis and development as possible. It is worthwhile noting, therefore, that a number of publications have occurred before the publication of this book dealing with the various aspects of leadership development covered in the last three chapters.

In April, 1978, **The Stages of Leadership Development** by Brian Hall was published in **Social Action,** April to June issue. Two other articles by Hall, Cantin, and Smith on the theory of the development of consciousness and its relationship to leadership were also published in a book called **The Politics of Change and Leadership Development: New Leaders in India and Africa.** This was edited by Alfred D'Souza and published by Manohar Press in 1978. Also, an article relating to the project in Seattle was published in Maury Smith's book, **A Practical Guide to Value Clarification,** which was a book on management and value clarification published by University Associates in 1977. Maury also contributed to the theory of development earlier as a consultant author in the initial value-clarification book published in 1973. Another publication on executive management was also published in India in 1979 by Manohar Press, collecting all the articles on leadership by Brian Hall for publication in India.

Finally, a large number of clientele are from ecclesiastical institutions. A yearly training session and internship for religious executives were run in Malta. Consequently in 1980, Paulist Press published **God's Plan For Us: A Practical Strategy for Communal Discernment of Spirits** by Brian Hall and Benjamin Tonna. This is the theory made explicit in terms understandable by religious executives.

In light of the purpose of this book, the value method has proven helpful during the last few years in terms of relating stages of development to urban planning and development, and to personnel and hiring. It has also proved helpful as a corporation compares its management objectives to the good of the society as a whole. This is especially important in terms of advertising and public relations.

Many of these practical aspects have not been included in this book because the purpose was to integrate all the research over the last few years, and to present fairly short and expressive statements of how we understand values develop in persons and organizations, particulary in relationship to leadership.

It was to this end that Dr. Helen Thompson has made a meaningful contribution by working closely with Hall on a number of these consultations and becoming intimately involved in the value process itself. Thus she was able to take all the research and all the writings and integrate them into this book. The purpose of this book then is to make as clear a statement as possible about Hall's theory so that other researchers and creative critics might build upon it. Finally, thanks to Gene Neidnagel for his editorial work and our present Vice President, Dr. Hal Taylor, for his criticism and introduction to the book in order to make it a more useful publication.

Dr. Brian Hall
Graduate Humanities,
University of Santa Clara
Santa Clara, California

Prologue

As mankind faces the twenty-first century, we are confronted with a critical choice. We can allow ourselves to be victimized by the oppression of bureaucratic institutions and uncontrolled technology. We can continue to exhaust and pollute our natural environment. Or, in response to a common call, we can begin to take authority for creation, and in cooperation with each other and with nature, we can build and renew the face of the earth. The latter alternative, the vision calling us to take authority cooperatively for creation, inspires and gives focus to our theme, "toward servant leadership."

Robert Greenleaf (1977) has ably described capable but caring individuals whose choice to serve has caused them to lead. Competent, caring persons can humanize our institutions and harness our technologies. In cooperation with others who care, they can seek to restore harmony to our natural world, to our inner worlds, and among our human communities. In an age of the anti-leader, we are haunted by the need for

leadership that this vision inspires, but appalled by the dearth of persons able and willing to respond to it. The pages that follow address this paradox.

Our initial chapter seeks insight from social scientists. What future realities confront organizational leaders at the executive level? Can administrative theory and research shed light on our concern for the development of servant leaders? In the second chapter, we present a theoretical framework based on the development of consciousness and values that we feel can be usefully applied to leadership development. Chapter III contains a description of seven leader-followership styles and addresses the processes by which a person moves through them. The fourth chapter examines the question of motivation. Why do some persons lead and others, who could, do not? Finally, in a brief epilogue we revisit leadership theory and research looking at it in terms of consciousness, value, and skill development.

Lest a person who does not perceive himself or herself as a potential servant leader, be tempted to read no further, we add this note. We are convinced that leadership style can never be separated from followership style. If the world's needs demand a servant-leadership style, then the world also needs persons who will follow only leaders who are servants. We invite present leaders, potential leaders, and persons who may always be followers to explore with us the vision that has inspired this book.

Chapter I

Leadership Theory and Skill Development

Future Realities. Men and women at the executive level of organizations confront their worlds of work with continually increasing pressure both from the external environment and from within their own corporate structures. Over a decade ago, Bennis (1968) described some of these new realities suggesting that solutions characteristic of authoritarian leadership no longer possessed the capability of solving the problems the future will thrust upon us.

Since innumerable futurists have already reported their prognosis about the years remaining to the twentieth century, we choose not to fill additional pages showing that the future will no longer reflect the past. We do however wish to

enumerate, with some modifications to Bennis's original list, those "new realities" that we believe will significantly affect the lives of leaders at the executive level.

1. We continue to face an era of increasingly rapid technological change.

2. We will experience world, national, and local events as turbulent and unpredictable rather than as anticipated and certain.

3. We are reaching the known limits to our present energy resources and the pollution limits of our natural environment.

4. We must accept and operate on a new concept of person, based on a deepened understanding of personality and the complexity of its needs.

5. We must accept and operate on a new concept of power based on collaboration rather than on coercion, on a democratic ethic rather than on autocratic practice.

6. Increasing volume, expanding markets, and diversification of products will make organizations increasingly more complex.

7. More complex organizations will experience greater difficulty in clarifying their goals and establishing an organizational identity.

8. The general educational level of all workers and the specialized training of professionals and technicians will rise and increase the need for interdependence.

9. The higher educational level of workers, the separation of management from ownership, the intervention of government, and the strength of unions will continue to force a broader distribution of power.

Bennis concludes that "the conditions of our modern industrial world will bring about the death of bureaucracy" (1969, p. 19) and goes on to describe organization of the future as "adaptive, problem-solving, temporary systems of diverse specialists, linked together by coordinating and task-evaluating executive specialists in an organic flux" (1969, p. 30).

Bennis is concerned with developing organizations that are "adaptive, problem-solving, temporary systems"; we are concerned with developing leaders who are "coordinating, task-evaluating, executive specialists." We seek to discover the conditions that enable persons in leadership positions to:

• Deal effectively with employees who require involvement, participation, and autonomy.

- Collaborate with highly trained specialists in technical, complicated and unprogrammed tasks.
- Direct the adaptive or innovative-creative capacity of businesses.
- Cope with conflicting, even contradictory, standards for organizational effectiveness.
- Facilitate the development of quick and intense personal relationships and bear the absence of more enduring work relationships.

In describing these tasks of the "executive specialist," Bennis (1969, p. 33ff) has defined some highly sophisticated personal skills essential to effective leadership within his proposed model. Bureaucracy, as an effective institutional structure, may be dying, but there is little reason to hope that from its ashes will rise fully formed executives capable of creatively coping with the demands of the "future realities." It is our conviction that effective leadership does not just happen; it can be developed.

Leadership Theory: A Historical Survey

Leadership theory and research provide insight into understanding the nature of leadership, but its very extensiveness and complexity also serve to confuse. For example, do we best understand leadership by focusing on the person of the leader, his traits and characteristics? Do we attempt to describe the leader's behavior? The leader's style? Should we look at the position, its role and function, its level of power within the organization? Should we also include the human environment in which the leader operates, the nature of the task he directs, the resulting interaction between the leader and the situational factors that surround him?

A survey of leadership theory also enables us to think about the development of leaders. We can anticipate that a current leadership theory will influence the practice of leadership training that follows it in time. In the next four sections we examine leadership theory and consequent training practice in terms of the personal skills that are implicitly expected in effective leaders. With the focus on the expected leader skills, we shall examine the contributions and limitations of task-oriented theory, of humanistic two-dimensional theories, and of situational theories. We shall consider the influence each of these has exerted on training for leadership and its usefulness in coping with the challenges confronting future organizational executives.

Efficiency and Productivity: Developing Instrumental Skills. During the first two decades of the twentieth century, the task of leadership was simple—to get the job done. Drucker (1969, p. 42) suggests that in society as well as in industry, this period was the "heroic age of the entrepreneur." "The inventors of this period had to know how to convert their technical work into economic performance and their invention into a business. It was then that the big businesses of today were founded." Leaders were born, not made! The leader was the individual whose technical skills could increase efficiency and productivity; his style was authoritarian; his organization, hierarchical and bureaucratic. Little or no attention was paid to the needs of the employee.

In his lecture "The Human Side of Enterprise," McGregor (1957) describes this conventional conception of management's task by stating a set of three propositions that he calls "Theory X":

> Management is responsible for organizing the elements of productive enterprise—money, materials, equipment, people—in the interest of economic ends.
>
> With respect to people, this is a process of directing their efforts, motivating them, controlling their actions, modifying their behavior to fit the needs of the organization.
>
> Without this active intervention by management, people would be passive —even resistant—to organizational needs. They must therefore be persuaded, rewarded, punished, controlled—their activities must be directed. (Vroom and Deci, 1970, pp. 307–308)

Management implicitly assumes that the worker is (1) indolent, one who works only when compelled, (2) dependent and prefers to be led, one lacking initiative and concern for corporate goals, (3) resistant to, even fearful of change, and (4) less intelligent than the leadership, a gullible person needing to be protected. At best "Theory X" attitudes ignore the individual; at worst, these attitudes become dehumanizing. While they pervaded the industrial era until recently, they are not uncommon today. However, many persons believe that such a stance is not only less human than that of which we are capable, but that a new consciousness has emerged making such practices impossible over an extended period of time.

16

Until recently leaders were "discovered," not "developed." The prevailing view claimed that different degrees of talent, energy, and persuasive force separated the leaders from the followers. The latter would always be led by the superior few. It was the "great-man" theory of leadership. If "great men" could be identified, it should be possible to distinguish those superior qualities that differentiated them from the less talented. The "trait theory of leadership" sugeested that organizations need only select as leaders those persons possessing the desired traits of personality and character.

However, as early as 1911, Taylor suggested that managers needed to be scientific in their approach. They must acquire specific technical skills essential to improving production and control systematically. The most sophisticated managers were educated within the context of higher education where schools of business developed cognitive skills related to productivity and management. Business-administration programs continue to place primary emphasis on professional or instrumental skills, although leadership theory has moved beyond this one-dimensional approach to management.

Humanistic Two-Dimensional Theories: Developing Interpersonal Skills. Following World War II, Hemphill (1950) and others began to look at the behavior of

an individual while he acted as a leader rather than at the personality traits of the leader. As a result of their empirical research, it became evident that the person perceived to be an effective leader focused his behavior around two concerns: (1) initiating structure in pursuit of organizational goals, and (2) considering the personal needs of individuals. Two-dimensioned theories have been further developed by Argyris, Likert, Blake and Mouton, and others. In addition to seeing leadership as two-dimensional, these researchers also make assumptions about people who are more humanistic. Although it is the nature of the organization to be structured and controlled, the human being is by nature a motivated organism.

McGregor (1957) explains this more humanistic attitude that he calls "Theory Y." Management is still responsible for organizing the elements of productive enterprise in the interest of economic ends, but to this initial proposition, McGregor adds three more:

People are **not** by nature passive or resistant to organizational needs. They have become so as a result of experience in organizations.

The motivation, the potential for development, the capacity for assuming responsibility, the readiness to direct behavior toward organizational goals are all present in people. Management does not put them there. It is a responsibility of management to make it possible for people to recognize and develop these human characteristics for themselves.

The essential task of management is to arrange organizational conditions and methods of operation so that people can achieve their own goals **best** by directing **their own** efforts toward organizational objectives. (Vroom and Deci, 1970, p. 315)

The humanistic, two-dimensional theories suggest that the effective leader is one who can integrate the achievement of organizational goals with the need-satisfaction of persons within the organization. Argyris (1964) believes that leaders must enable followers to make a creative contribution to the organization as a natural outgrowth of their needs to growth and self-expression. "Enabling" others demands well-developed interpersonal skills. Likert (1967) is even more specific about the interpersonal skills expected of the effective leader:

The leader must present behaviors and organizational processes perceived by followers as supportive of their efforts and of their sense of personal worth. He will involve followers in making decisions that affect their welfare and work. He will use his influence in order to further task performance and personal welfare of followers. The leader builds group cohesiveness and motivation for productivity by providing freedom for responsible decision-making and exercise of initiative. (Stodgill, 1974, p. 22)

Clearly the democratic style described here demands that the leader possess highly developed interpersonal skills. The "managerial grid" designed by Blake and Mouton (1964) provides a useful model for visualizing the two-dimensional theories. Illustrated in Figure 1.1, the grid consists of two, nine-point axes: (1) concern for people and (2) concern for production.

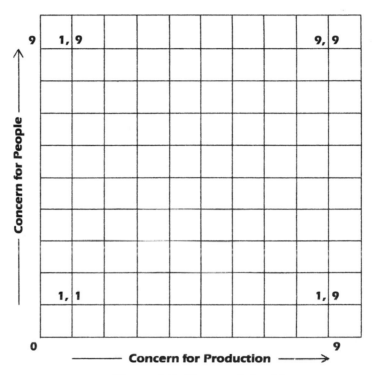

Figure 1.1: Managerial grid.

According to Blake and Mouton, a leader may be low on both dimensions, (1,1); high on one, low on the other, (1,9 or 9,1); or high on both (9,9).

The managerial grid suggests the shift in leadership training from that focused exclusively on concern for production to a focus that also includes concern for human relations. Unfortunately, most human-relations training programs focus exclusively on that factor. The most widespread program, sensitivity training groups and its variants, comes in for serious criticism. On the one hand, it

19

purports to develop democratic leadership style, but in fact its methodology creates a course of training in laissez-faire behavior. Stodgill (1974, p. 199) claims that it is

> a contradiction of fact to call sensitivity training a method for building leadership. It is effective for its stated purpose of training in the "democratic" sharing of leadership with followers; however, it is misnomer to call the resulting pattern of behavior a form of democratic leadership.

Perhaps a more accurate criticism of sensitivity training lies less in what it actually does—sensitize individuals to the inner world of human emotion—and more in what its users expect it to accomplish—train leaders. Well done, sensitivity training can develop interpersonal skills, skills clearly missing from leadership style that is authoritarian and bureaucratic. But leadership, even democratic leadership, is not the exclusive domain of interpersonal activity.

Leadership as "Origination"; Skills of the Imagination.
To this point in our discussion, we have used the terms "leader" and "manager" interchangeably. Katz and Kahn raise an interesting issue by suggesting that "leadership" should be distinguished from "management." They "consider the essence of organizational leadership to be the influential increment over and above the mechanical compliance with the routine directives of the organization" (1966, p. 312). According to these authors, this "influential increment" is present on the basis of different types of power one may hold or on the effective influence one may exert. Clearly the president of a nation has types and levels of power different from an executive at General Motors. Or, two persons at the same level in an organization who possess equal power may not exert equal influence within the organization. If we were to make the concept of "influential increment" more explicit, we might state that management elicits the minimum acceptable behavior while leadership elicits the "something more"—the increment.

Katz and Kahn make a further useful distinction. They refer to three types of leadership processes: (1) origination, (2) interpolation, and (3) administration. Administration requires technical knowledge and an understanding of how the system operates. It might be equated with the concept "management" where the minimal acceptable behavior demands instrumental skills of technical competence. Interpolation is characteristic of leadership at the intermediate level of subsystem or division where skill in human relations is essential. The "influential increment" that distinguishes interpolation from administration might be described as the development and use of interpersonal skills. Finally, origination is characteristic of leadership at the top echelons where the leader needs a total-systems perspective and probably some charismatic qualities. Katz and Kahn (1966, p. 313) refer to the "intellective aspect of leadership" required of origination leadership:

> Everyone who has lived the organizational life has experienced the difference among individuals in their ability to see, conceptualize, appraise, predict, and understand the demands and opportunities posed to the organization by its environment. Yet the intellective aspect of leadership has been neglected in research. Persuasiveness, warmth and interpersonal skills are frequently urged as the essentials of leadership, but to what end? If a leader is seriously mistaken about the systemic requirements of his organization or the demands of the environment, his interpersonal abilities may become organizational liabilities.

It would seem that "the intellective aspect of leadership" has not only been neglected in research, but also in the training of leaders. It would seem that "the intellective aspect" is something more than the instrumental, cognitive skills of professional management. Katz and Kahn seem to point to the skills of the imagination, to creativity, to the ability to intuit, to the process of synergy——the joining together of apparently irrelevant elements. Only when these skills are developed can the leader see "the systemic requirements of his organization" and the future "demands of the environment." At the highest levels of leadership effective system skills are dependent upon well developed imaginal skills.

Unfortunately, the development of leadership at this level is seriously neglected. Most trainingPprograms are directed toward lower and middle management. The criticism about a lack of leadership in our day is made more in relation to leadership as origination rather than leadership as interpolation or administration. Perhaps the real issue is whether training for origination leadership is possible. If so, under what conditions can it occur? Under what conditions can the creative imagination of leaders be developed?

The Situation Surrounding a Leader: Envisioning the System. While the two-dimensional theories have "humanized" leadership by focusing attention on the "people" factor as well as the "production" factor, they fail to take into account the environment in which specific persons are organized to perform specific tasks. Using essentially the same dimensions labeled "task behavior" and "relationship behavior," Hersey and Blanchard (1969) have added a third dimension—"group psychological maturity"—which takes into consideration the human environment in which the leader operates. Perhaps the most completely developed situational theory has been proposed by Fiedler (1967) who looks at the "favorableness of the situation" in relationship to the leader's personality, behavior, and style. Recognizing the maturity level of the group, the nature of the task, the overall milieu in which the leader-follower interaction takes place enables us to get a better handle on the "systems" within and among which the leader operates.

In their "life-cycle theory," Hersey and Blanchard propose that "group psychological maturity" determines appropriate leader behavior. The psychological maturity of the group can be estimated from (1) its capacity and willingness to set high but attainable goals, (2) its willingness and ability to assume responsibility for performance, and (3) its educational and experience levels. As these factors increase, appropriate leader-behavior must also change to meet the demands of the group's more mature level. In other words as the maturity or consciousness level of the worker-group expands, the group requires different treatment by its leaders until, ultimately, it requires no treatment at all.

While this "life-cycle" is an ideal for conceptualizing group development, the nature and conditions of the work may significantly affect its progress and may even arrest its development. For example, an assembly line denies the work group any opportunity for the development of all three factors identified by Hersey and Blanchard. The **goals** are pre-set when the speed of the line is established regardless of the workers' willingness to assume responsibility. **Responsibility** has been pre-empted by the programming engineers and **experience** is limited to those few discreet tasks programmed into each position. The assembly line is a mechanization of McGregor's Theory X and appropriate leader-behavior is fixed at high-task orientation and low-relationship orientation.

The sales force of an organization or the construction trades that emphasize competition, measurability of performance, and interpersonal support require leader-behavior that is high on both task and relationship. In a broader sense it is the world of professional athletes, beribboned generals, and gray-flannel suits. It is a world populated by Vince Lombardi and George Patton. Individual performance is required, but for the good of the "team." For Blake and Mouton it is "9,9 Management," the "team" quadrant on their "managerial grid."

Architectural firms, engineering groups, professional organizations as well as the skilled operators of highly mechanized industry such as continuous process petro-chemical production illustrate a third type work-situation. These are maturing employees who know their work well, do it for its intrinsic reward, and require more social support than task direction. These situations suggest that appropriate leader-behavior would be more relationship oriented than task oriented. Unfortunately organizational-development literature is replete with cases where the leader-behavior was reversed—task oriented rather than relationship oriented, the result of which is high turbulance among personnel.

A final and less frequent type work-situation lies in the realm of creativity—the "think-tank," the research laboratory, the artisan group. Productive output can be anticipated only in its broadest terms; scientific discovery, creative insight can be facilitated but not directed. Management provides the physical facilities and pays the bills; leadership is collegial-sharing and peer-criticism. To the businessman, the creative world appears nonproductive under nonleadership. Leadership has become plural and virtually invisible.

Following the "life-cycle theory" through four distinctive types of work situations suggests some interesting comparisons. In each case the "appropriate leader-behavior" differed. Leadership was high task, low relationship on the assembly line; high task, high relationship with the Green Bay Packers under Lombardi; low task, high relationship in the law firm; and low task, low relationship among the creative thinkers. The four illustrations suggest quadrants similar to, but in effect quite different from, the managerial grid of Blake and Mouton. Figure 1.2 superimposes the "life-cycle quadrants"—the inner shaded area—on the four quadrants of the managerial grid—the outer white area—with some quite striking implications for the appropriateness of the leader-behavior. Perhaps there are situations where the maturity and skill development of the workers in combination with the nature of the task demand that appropriate leader-behavior emphasize task, people, both, or neither. A 9,9 management may well be appropriate for businesses built on the values of capitalistic enterprise, but it becomes increasingly less appropriate as the skill level of the workers becomes more sophisticated and their motivation becomes more internalized and intrinsic to the work they do. Leader-behavior characteristic of a Vince Lombardi on a gridiron is ineffective and inappropriate in a law firm or "think tank."

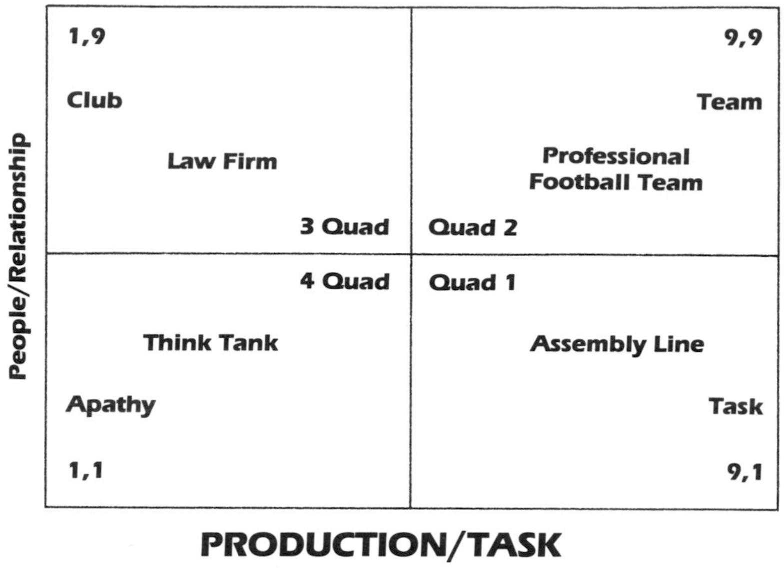

PRODUCTION/TASK
Figure 1.2:—Life-cycle quadrants superimposed on the managerial grid.

Although there are many interaction theories relating leadership style to followership style, Sweney and Fiechtner (1973) have identified three dominant leader-follower roles that tend to follow a pattern of maturation on the part of both leaders and followers. These researchers suggest that organizations are sustained by diametrically opposed behavior patterns on the part of those in superordinate and subordinate roles. The authoritarian leader who **retains power** depends on ingratiating followers who **respect power.** The permissive leader who **denies power to himself** depends upon the rebel who **seeks power for himself.** The egalitarian leader who **shares power** needs cooperators with whom to **share power.** The evidence suggests that organizations are most effectively sustained by the egalitarian-cooperator roles which according to the criteria proposed by Hersey and Blanchard demand a higher level of psychological maturity than the authoritarian ingratiator or permissive-rebel roles.

Finally, it is possible to look not at the work-task of the group in relationship to appropriate leader-behavior, but rather at the tasks expected of leaders at various levels within an organization. Clement and Ayres (1976), based on earlier work by Clement and Zierdt (1975), have identified nine subsets of leadership skills that have been associated with five organizational levels of leadership—first-line supervisor, low-level management, middle management, executive, and policy maker. As Figure 1.3 demonstrates, skills of technical competence and supervision—instrumental and interpersonal skills—are needed more at lower levels of the organization than at the higher levels. Those skills of planning, decision-making and ethical climate-setting—imaginal and systems skills—increase at the higher level. Skills of administration and management that tend to be interpersonal skills dominate the middle levels. The skills associated with the various levels of leadership bear a marked similarity to the leadership processes suggested by Katz and Kahn: administration, interpolation, and origination.

Level of Leadership	First-line Supervisor	Low-level Management	Middle Management	Executive	Policy-maker
Leadership Skills					
Technical Skills					
Supervision					
Communications					
Human Relations					
Counseling					
Management Science					
Ethics					
Planning					
Decision-Making					

Figure 1.3:—Matrix of organizational leadership: Leadership skills and levels of leadership.

In addition to identifying the skills expected at each level of leadership, Clement and Ayres suggest that the character of the skill changes as the position in the organization rises. For example, communication at the lower levels is primarily transmitting verbal messages face-to-face from supervisor to worker. At mid-level management, written communications are sent from office to office. At the highest level every action on the part of an executive or policy-maker is, in itself, a communication diligently noted by the entire work-force. Planning also changes in character from the lowest level where it might include work-scheduling to the top level where planning might mean "visionary environmental articulation."

25

The work of Clement and Ayres strongly suggests that the character change in the skills expected of leadership as it moves from lower to higher levels within the organization follows a pattern similar to the "life-cycle curve" of Hersey and Blanchard. That is to say, the nature of the leadership tasks as leadership positions move from lower levels to higher levels follows a pattern of change similar to the four quadrants illustrated in Figure 1.2 above. This pattern of change is predictable from the criteria of maturity proposed by Hersey and Blanchard and from an understanding of the expectations of leadership at the higher levels of a bureaucracy. It also suggests that within complex organizations a requirement exists for various forms of leadership. At the top of an organizational hierarchy it is the nature of the leadership task, rather than the task of the organization, that is more significant. These leadership tasks must be effectively achieved for the organization to sustain itself. Perhaps this explains why a chief executive of a major newspaper can easily become the president of a major airline.

In looking for ways that contemporary executives might learn the systems skills essential to effective leadership at the

highest levels, we are tempted to focus on the strategies of organization development (OD). Clearly organization development is the most sophisticated effort to effect change within an institution. As an educational strategy, it nearly always focuses on the "people variable" rather than on the goals, structure, or work of the organization. It is experience-based; it processes human emotion; but it is not simply sensitivity training. According to Bennis (1969, p. 77) perhaps OD's foremost theorist-practitioner,

> organization development is a response to complex challenges, an educational strategy which aims to bring about a better fit between the human beings who work in and expect things from organizations and the busy, unrelenting environment with its insistence on adapting to changing times.

While recognizing the worth of OD, both for the institution and its individuals who particpate in its processes, it must be noted that its primary concern is to bring about planned **organizational** change. It is not an **individual** development program. Blake and Mouton (1969, p. vi) make this observation and follow it by an interesting note:

> Because of the history of education, training, and development in industry, the inclination on seeing the word **organization** before **development** is to think and substitute for it the word **individual.** If the reader does this, he will miss the deeper implication of what is presented. The reason is that he will fail to comprehend how deeply the culture of a corporation controls the behavior of all of its individuals. While the ultimate objective of organization development is to liberate all of the individuals within it, so that they will be free, participative, and contributive to problem solving, in order to achieve corporate purposes of profitability, this objective cannot be reached until the constraints that operate within the corporation's culture have been studied and deliberately rejected.

Top-level executives whose organization participates in an organization-development process might further develop their systems skills. However, it is unlikely that an organization would undertake this process with that purpose in mind. As with the case of developing the skills of the imagination, there appear to be few opportunities for individuals consciously to develop systems skills.

Summary

It was the intent of this chapter to examine the history of leadership theory with the focus on the personal skills expected of the effective leader. We then looked to leadership-training programs that might enable persons to develop these skills. In the course of this journey, we analyzed the one-dimensional view of bureaucratic management that focuses exclusively on the goals-work-productivity of an organization. We considered humanistic, two-dimensional theories that recognize the individual as a person who, when motivated, could contribute significantly to the goals of the organization. Finally we looked at situational theories that add an environmental dimension, including concepts such as the maturity of the group and the nature of the work. From this review of leadership theory, five factors emerge that we believe are significant dimensions for the holistic development of leaders in the future:

1. The effective leader will integrate the needs of the group with the goals of the organization. See the humanistic two-dimensional theories of Hemphill, McGregor, Blake and Mouton, and others.

2. A leader's concern for persons will be manifest in appropriate behavior when the leader takes into account the group's psychological maturity. See the life-cycle theory of Hersey and Blanchard.

3. A leader's concern for the person and concern for the product will be manifest in appropriate behavior when the leader takes into account the situational milieu including the nature of the task as well as the maturity level of the group. See the contingency theory of Fiedler.

4. To sustain the leader-follower relationship over time, the leadership style will mirror-image the style required by the followership. Styles of followership tend to follow the pattern of a group's psychological maturity. See Sweney and Fiechtner.

5. As the levels of leadership within an organization move from lower to higher positions, the skills required appear to undergo a character change following a pattern similar to the "life-cycle curve" of Hersey and Blanchard. At the executive level, the nature of the leadership task is more significant than the task of the organization. See Clement and Ayres.

The Four Kinds of Skills

In reviewing the history of leadership theory, we referred to four different types of skills: (1) instrumental skills associated with work and productivity, (2) interpersonal skills needed to deal with the human side of enterprise, (3) imaginal skills, and (4) systems skills required by the nature of the leadership task at the executive level.

Elsewhere (Hall, 1976) we have described at length the genesis of skills according to the four categories enumerated above. We recognize that other divisions of skills are useful and valid, but for our purposes, we believe a brief explanation of these categories will facilitate a better understanding of skills applied to levels of leadership. **Instrumental skills** are task-oriented. They encampass those abilities an individual possesses and on which he can rely to get a job done. They cover the very general skills needed by the general population within a culture; they cover the professional and technical skills required of the specialist. They include reading and writing, using a pipet, performing brain surgery, designing and using tools. These skills may be cognitive or physical or a combination of both. Instrumental skills, then, are

the peculiar blend of intelligence and manual dexterity that enables one to be professional and competent . . . the ability to manipulate ideas and the immediate external environment . . . the skill of handicrafts, physical dexterity and cognitive accomplishment.

Human growth is dependent on the development of **interpersonal skills** that equip an individual to enter into satisfying human relationships. There is a noticeable correlation between a person's expansion of consciousness and a widening of his social relationships. To increase the radius of his social sphere and also to intensify and deepen existing relationships a person must acquire special kinds of skills. Basic interpersonal skills can be described in terms of some specific components as well as obstacles to their use. For example, general **communication** is based not only on the ability to verbalize but also on one's sense of worth and confidence. A lack of trust in others, a lack of imagination, or a fear of disapproval obstruct the communication process. **Listening** demands attentiveness to others and the ability to concentrate. It can be thwarted by excessive preoccupation with self. **To be in touch with one's own feelings** involves the ability to listen to emotions, to appreciate them as valuable sources of information, to use them constructively. **Empathy** includes a sensitivity to the feelings of another, the ability to identify with another, an objective mental attitude. A lack of imagination is an obstacle to empathy. At a more sophisticated level, **caring** involves openness, availability, and pain tolerance. The need to control others inhibits caring. **Intimacy** includes a tolerance for self-disclosure, conflict capability, and emotional warmth. Interpersonal skills include

> the ability to act with generosity and understanding towards others that flows from a knowledge of oneself . . . the ability to objectify one's own feelings so that cooperation rather than isolation is enhanced.

To understand **imaginal skills** we must recognize the synergetic interaction among fantasy, the emotions, and the reflective intellect. We must recognize that the imagination is not three things but an integrated whole. Fantasy refers to the operation of the imagination that uses psychic energy to convert data, received from either the external environment or one's inner world, into images. This image-making ability, while natural to all men, is more developed in some people than in others. The emotions, then, evaluate the data, perceiving them as helpful or harmful, desirable or to be avoided. Only rarely are data perceived as neutral. The emotions evaluate and pass judgment on the images created by the fantasy. The reflective intellect examines and organizes the data, picked up from the environment and evaluated by the emotions, with a view to simplifying them and constructing an idea. One key activity of the reflective intellect, so typical of creative people, is the ability to conjure up and to consider alternative ways of dealing with information. For this reason, imagination is often described as the faculty that enables an individual to see alternatives to reality as presently constituted.

Imaginal skills include a wide range of abilities: for example, the ability to fantasize and create new alternatives, to see the consequences of the alternatives and to prioritize the more productive ones; the ability to criticize and evaluate situations and to read their potential and limitations. Imaginal skills include the

> peculiar blend of internal fantasy and feeling that enables us to externalize our ideas in an effective and practical manner . . . the ability to see and make sense out of increasing amounts of data . . . the capacity to learn from direct experience, to choose and to act on complex alternatives creatively.

Systems skills involve the integration and use of instrumental, imaginal, and interpersonal skills as the individual relates to his social world. They include such skills as the ability to synthesize complex data, statements, and emotional input received from within and outside the organization; the ability to make sense of apparently disparate data; the ability to differentiate, within a small group, interpersonal needs and systems needs. Systems skills include

> that peculiar blend of imagination, sensitivity and competence which gives rise to the capacity to see all the parts of a system as they relate to the whole system . . . to the ability to plan and design change in that system so as to maximally enhance the growth of the individual persons and parts of the organization.

Conclusion

The foregoing analysis—of leadership theory and of leadership skills—seems to suggest that an adequate model for leadership development must include (1) an understanding of the total work environment, and (2) a recognition of an array of appropriate leader behaviors. An understanding of the total work environment must consider the personal needs that are meaningful at the maturity level of the group and that are consistent with the nature of the task. In recognizing an array of appropriate leader behaviors, we acknowledge not only the interdependence of leadership-followership styles, but we also suggest (1) that leadership-followership styles are related to maturity level, and (2) that these styles are related to the level in the organization of the leadership position. Maturity appears to be a significant factor in differentiating appropriate leader behavior and in identifying potential leadership in individuals. Therefore, we believe that a developmental model of human growth can provide a useful framework for understanding leadership and for training persons for leadership positions at various levels.

Chapter II

A Theory of Consciousness and Value Developmen

Hall's theory of consciousness and value development posits that, in their quest for meaning, human beings construct a perception of their "world" and an image of their "self" functioning effectively in that world. It posits that the "contents" of these "world views" and "images of the self" differ significantly as an individual matures. From experience it appears that four significantly distinct phases of consciousness can be identified. These phases can be identified in the natural pattern of growth from childhood through maturity. They can be identified in the history of a people or in the development of a culture. It appears that the phases of consciousness are

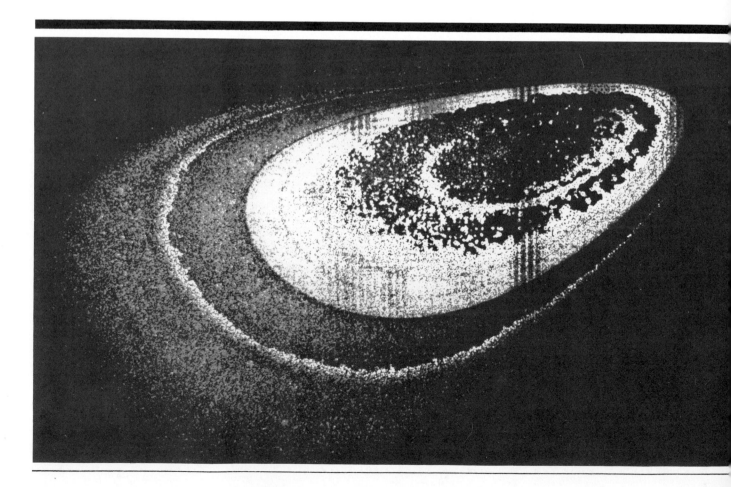

developmental; that is, their sequence is ordered and irreversible. The person must satisfactorily experience each previous phase as an essential prerequisite for imagining the possibility of and then moving into a subsequent phase. However, an individual who has experienced a subsequent phase of consciousness may be forced, by the oppressiveness of the environment or by his own anxiety, to readopt behavior characteristic of an earlier phase.

The behavior characteristic of a phase of consciousness is determined by three factors: 1) how the world is perceived by the individual; 2) how the individual perceives the self functioning within that world; and 3) what human needs the self seeks to satisfy. Put another way, the self will function in response to the perceived pressures imposed by the external environment and in response to the felt human needs that impel from within. When the perceived environmental expectations change, and when the inner felt needs of the individual change, then the behavior of the individual changes. Implicit in an individual's behavior are the values that motivate and give priority to his activities, and the skills associated with the experience of his successful performance. Briefly, then, Hall's theory of consciousness and value development implies that the acquisition of quite specific skills is associated with each phase of consciousness. It also implies that quite specific human values can be associated with each of the four phases.

The theory of consciousness development is descriptive not prescriptive. It arises from observation and experience. Each phase can be easily described and readily understood by an ordinary observer of human behavior. In the following sections, the phases of consciousness will be described in terms of their general characteristics: the perception of the world, the image of the self, and the felt human needs. They will be illustrated by examples from the pattern of an individual's growth, from the history of a culture or civilization, or from contemporary adult behavior.

The Phases of Consciousness and Value Development

Phase One Consciousness. The world in Phase One is perceived as a mystery over which the individual has no control. It is a hostile world in which the self merely exists, but the self exists at the center of its world. The self struggles to survive in this alien, capricious environment. For the child, it is a new world, a mystery to which the self responds with wonder and awe. During the initial phase of consciousness, the individual seeks to satisfy physical human needs; the need for food, for warmth; the need for shelter and for sexual pleasure. Self-preservation and security motivate the individual to acquire the skills that will guarantee his safety and insure his survival.

In his early life, the child experiences a mysterious world in which he is the center. He is need-oriented, very physical, and totally dependent. He values his own security and all that contributes to his bodily well-being. But he also responds to the beauty of his mysterious new world with wonder and awe. In **Alice in Wonderland,** Lewis Carroll captures the fanciful delight in the young child's response to his self-centered world. The dialogue at the Mad Hatter's Tea Party illustrates the child's world where everything is related to his own delight.

> The table was a very large one, but the three were all crowded together in one corner of it.
>
> "No room! No room!" they cried out when they saw Alice coming.
>
> "There is plenty of room!" said Alice indignantly, as she sat down in a large armchair at one end of the table.
>
> "Have some wine," the March Hare said in an encouraging tone.
>
> Alice looked around the table, but there was nothing on it but tea. "I don't see any wine," she remarked.
>
> "There isn't any," said the March Hare.
>
> "Then it wasn't very civil of you to offer it," says Alice angrily.
>
> "It wasn't very civil of you to sit down without being invited," says the March Hare.
>
> "I didn't know it was your table," says Alice; "It's laid for a great many more than three."
>
> "Your hair wants cutting," said the Hatter. He had been looking at Alice for some time with great curiosity, and this was his first speech.

Like the small child, A. A. Milne's (1961) Winnie the Pooh enjoyed an egocentric world that was there just for him. Pooh loves honey; so when the hungry little bear sees a bee, he says to himself "If I follow the bee to the tree, I will find honey for me." Piaget's descriptions of preoperational thought also suggest the self-centeredness of the small child's perception of the world. For a four-year-old, a lake may be defined as "the place where I go in the summer."

Many middle-class American children may only moderately experience their world as an alien environment, especially if their physical needs are satisfied almost instantly. However, the children of poverty, young victims of oppression and war, and youngsters who grow up in a ghetto all experience the full impact of a hostile world in which a very young self must fight to survive.

Myth-making and ceremonial ritual, surrounding phenomena of nature characteristic of primitive cultures, illustrate the Phase One wonder-awe response to the world as mystery. For more than a millennium Western man viewed the universe from his earthly vantage point that he perceived to be the center of all things. Ptolemy's geocentric world view was finally replaced by the heliocentric theory of Copernicus, but only after the theory was denounced by Protestant leaders as contrary to Scripture and by the Roman Inquisition as erroneous, if not heretical! Human beings seem to surrender self-centered world views only with considerable reluctance.

The struggle to survive in an alien hostile world can be variously illustrated. The American frontier was won by white men who perceived the wilds of the West and the wiles of its Indians as enemies to be conquered. The robber barons of American industry waged economic war in their fight to the financial "top." Jews who survived the German "Holocaust" suffered the ignominious, even demonic effort to eliminate a race or to reduce its living members systematically to the tragedy and horror of a Phase One existence. Living in the Uganda of Idi Amin, in the desert of Saudi Arabia, in American slums, and in too many inner-city schools, persons experience Phase One consciousness and evidence corresponding behavior.

But Phase One behavior is not limited to persons confined to obviously oppressive environments. Much American advertising appeals to adults who buy products based on Phase One values. Sex images, totally irrelevant to the quality of the product, "sell" most cigarettes, much liquor, and many automobiles. Spy movies and TV detective stories capitalize on Phase One attitudes toward life. A typical example is the popular television series from England called "The Protectors." The introductions to this half-hour spy thriller all begin in the same way. First, the viewer hears dramatic music followed by a picture of the hero tucking a revolver into his belt. The gun symbolizes survival; the hero is at war. But he is well-dressed and affluent, held in high esteem by government officials. In the next scene a car roars down the street, turns a corner, rolls over and bursts into flames. These symbols of danger force the viewer to fear for his own survival! Thereupon, the hero is seen beating eggs, eating a hearty breakfast, and walking down the street with a beautiful woman. Danger, war, and survival; physical gratification through food and sex; excitement and wonder are all dimensions of a Phase One way of life.

A Phase One life-style is not limited to the literature of the contemporary TV screen. Quite to the contrary. Classical and Shakespearean tragedy both build on an adult consciousness level characteristic of Phase One. Euripedes' Electra, with her brother Orestes, seeks to avenge the death of their father whose murder had been plotted by his unfaithful wife and their mother. This theme is still found in fantasies of our own time—the fairy tale of Snow White and the Seven Dwarfs. It may also be found in the fact of our times where children of an earlier marriage can unconsciously seek to "destroy" the parent who has remarried.

Phase Two Consciousness. In Phase Two the world is no longer perceived as hostile and alien, but rather it is a peopled world to which the self must belong and in which the self must succeed. Rather than a mystery over which the self has no control, the social world is a problem with which the individual can cope. The individual learns to do things that merit the approval of persons who are significant, thereby guaranteeing acceptance into the group and enhancing one's own sense of competence and confidence. By conforming to the norms of significant persons and groups and by becoming usefully productive, the self satisfies its social needs for acceptance, affirmation, approval, and achievement. By experiencing belonging and success, the self comes to realize a sense of self-worth.

The infant joins his social world by winning the approval of his parents and the acceptance of his family. As a small child he begins to venture out of "our home" onto "our block" into "our neighborhood" and finally into its school where he learns to read, to write, and to do arithmetic—the basic skills upon which personal competence and success will be built in "our society." What the child learns to do in order that he might belong varies radically across cultures, but basically the socialization process follows a similar pattern of (1) identifying with significant groups and (2) adopting behavior—learning skills—expected by the group for its members. As a consequence of a child's identifying with a "we" he also begins to identify the "they"—the other, the rival, the enemy.

As the middle-class American child grows, memberships increase—Little League, Brownies and Cub Scouts, Four H Clubs. Associated with school life are a variety of extra-curricular group activities—most typically organized sports. These organized activities share two characteristics in common: (1) to belong the youngster must live or play by the rules and (2) to succeed the youngster must demonstrate personal achievement. Belonging and success are celebrated in initiation rites and rites of passage both secular and sacred—induction ceremonies, graduations, bar mitzvah rites.

As a consequence of these types of experiences, the world that enters the individual's consciousness is one established by others into which he must fit himself if he is to experience a sense of personal worth. Self-esteem is achieved by becoming a useful participant in the regular activity of the existing order and by meeting the expectations of significant others, first one's family and peers, and then established institutions. In a world perceived as established and run by others, a person must play by the accepted rules. Authority is always external to the individual who sees the world as being controlled by "them." For the child, "they" tend to be parents and teachers and policemen. For the adult, "they" can be individuals—bosses, bishops, politicians, or groups—the neighbors, "the Joneses," even faceless members of a crowd. "They" can mean institutions—the church, the government, the company, or even abstractions—"law and order," "the way we have always done it," "what TV commercials tell us to do."

To become a useful participant in this world, the individual must contribute in a productive way to society's well-being. Personal meaning is acquired less through the satisfaction of the senses and more through the experience of cooperation in a worthwhile enterprise. Work as productive labor is valued because it provides the individual with a conviction that he is useful and that he has earned his right to belong. Approval by significant others and one's own awareness of being skilled produce in the individual a sense of self-worth.

The seventeenth-century Newtonian laws of physics, which ruled the world of science until recently, illustrate Phase Two consciousness. An established order exists in the universe that is governed by recognizable laws. When applied, these laws produce predictable results. Laws, when respected and used, make life stable and secure. As in the physical order, so also in the social order.

The American social order in the post-war fifties provides a more contemporary illustration of a world view characteristic of Phase Two. The Japanese surrender marked the end of Axis hostilities. The oppression of rationing and price control was eliminated. Economic stability lost during the Great Depression had been restored and the predictable laws of capitalism began following their established pattern of growth.

Suburbia, USA, mushroomed around every major metropolis. The organization man in his gray-flannel suit commuting home to his bedroom community could enjoy the self-esteem accruing to a "useful participant" in the existing order, approved by his boss, respected by his neighbors, and loved by his wife and children. In his garage were parked two cars; in his living room Madison Avenue filled his TV screen with those not-so-hidden persuaders telling him and his family what every member of the affluent society should have. The inner-directed man needs to achieve in a competitive society; the other-directed man needs to be affirmed in a corporate society—two dimensions of Phase Two consciousness.

On college campuses, the fifties saw the "few," acceptable to those who already belonged, fill sorority and frat houses. Sorority members vied to elect one of their sisters Homecoming Queen to reign over that autumn ceremonial

usually centered about a gridiron classic where highly skilled behemoths defended Alma Mater against her arch-rival. The entire Homecoming ritual is built on the social need to belong. With the successful orbiting of Sputnik, academic life grew more serious. "They"—the enemy—had won the first lap of the space race. To regain our position against our technological competition, the United States needed engineers highly competent in the fields of math and science. As the fifties waned, study groups began the revision of math and science curricula and more serious scholarship replaced the social whirl in college life. Again, the pair of Phase Two priorities reversed themselves—competence and achievement took priority over acceptance and belonging.

Although the general American mood has changed significantly since 1960, many Phase Two attitudes are prevalent in society today. Civilization is built on an established order that operates predictably. Personal growth is predicated on the affirmation and acceptance of significant others. All societies depend upon cooperative effort in productive enterprise; however, a problem can arise for an individual who is working through Phase Two consciousness if the society in which he lives overemphasizes Phase Two values. If too much emphasis is placed on success and production, the person may conclude that self-worth comes only from work. This kind of distortion sees competence in work as the only way to achieve a sense of belonging. **Nog's Vision** (Hall, 1974) a fairy tale about Pricklies, describes a distorted world where a work ethic alone prevailed.

Another odd thing about Pricklies was that they all came in different colors depending on what their job was. A Pricklie's job was the most important thing in the world to him. It was so important, in fact, that a Pricklie's job was what his name was.

The King was white with red pricklies and he was called—well, King Pricklie. He was the only red and white Pricklie in the land. The three king advisors were grey and, yes, they were called Advisor Pricklies.

There were several Doctor Pricklies. They were all white and sat all day in the hospital making babies and putting casts on broken Pricklies. Those who were pink wrote newspapers or made movies and television shows; they were called Telepricklies. All the brown Pricklies were policemen, and they kept law and order and made sure no foreigners came into the valley. The Pricklies who built the buildings were silver, while purple Pricklies made clothing for Pricklies to wear. Food was grown by green Pricklies.

It was a most pleasant land. Everybody knew his place. Everybody did something. In fact, everybody was quite, quite satisfied. But it had not always been that way.

You see, many, many years ago when the first Pricklies lived, they weren't quite so satisfied. They were so prickly it was difficult to make friends with each other. Why, Pricklies couldn't kiss or even shake hands because their pricklies got in the way. So over the years they learned not to sit close to each other.

The Transition to Phase Three. In the mainstream of American culture the shift in consciousness from Phase One to Phase Two frequently appears in the process of personal development. Within American life-styles, distinct phases of consciousness may be recognized in the world view, attitudes, and values that distinguish the secure social world of the middle class from the more alien, hostile environment perceived by persons who are victims of poverty or racial oppression. Similarly, Phases One and Two account for differences in attitudes and values between developing and developed nations. Although basically different in content, both Phases One and Two are highly visible in society and can be readily illustrated. They also possess a common "authority" dimension that radically differentiates them from the next two phases. In addition, Phases Three and Four are less visible and less readily illustrated. Therefore, we pause here to review what we have said about the development of consciousness and to reflect on the place of authority in the four phases.

One dimension in the process of human development is the individual's effort to give meaning to his self and to his world. John Gardner describes this meaning-making process in **Self Renewal: The Individual and the Innovative Society** (1964, p. 102):

Man has throughout history shown a compelling need to arrive at conceptions of the universe **in terms of which he could regard his own life as meaningful.** He wants to know where **he** fits into the scheme of things. He wants to understand how the great facts of the objective world relate to **him** and what they imply for his behavior. He wants to know what significance may be found in his own existence, the succeeding generations of his kind and the vivid events of his inner life. He seeks some kind of meaningful framework in which to understand (or at least to reconcile himself to) the indignities of chance and circumstance and the fact of death. . . . He seeks conceptions of the universe that give dignity, purpose and sense to his own existence.

To Gardner's description of man's "conception of the universe that gives him dignity, purpose and sense," Hall's theory adds the notion that these "conceptions" change with time according to a predictable pattern of development. We have described the first two phases in the development of consciousness. A common characteristic of these phases lies in the place of authority in relation to the individual. Authority is always external to the self, that is, the individual "adapts" to his environment. He passively accepts, conforms, seeks external approval, and relies on the direction of others. In contrast to "adaptation" characteristic of both Phase One and Two, Paulo Freire (1971) identifies an alternative to this pattern of behavior that he calls "integration."

> **Integration** with one's context, as distinguished from **adaptation,** is a distinctively human activity. Integration results from the capacity to adapt oneself to reality **plus** the critical capacity to make choices and transform that reality. To the extent that man loses his ability to make choices and is subjugated to the choices of others, to the extent that his decisions are no longer his own because they result from external prescriptions, he is no longer integrated. Rather, he has adapted. **(Education for Cultural Consciousness.)**

"Integration" describes a pattern of behavior characteristic of Phases Three and Four where authority has become internal to the self, that is, the individual uses **his** critical capacity to make choices and transform his environment. At Phase Two man

> has become free from the external bonds that would prevent him from doing and thinking as he sees fit. He would become free to act according to his own will, if he knew what **he** wanted, thought and felt. But he does not know. He conforms to anonymous authorities and adopts a self which is not his. (Italics ours. Fromm, 1941.)

But critical choice is more frequently obstructed by things "found in the mind rather than in external arrangements." Persons who are products of a highly organized society can become victims of "the crusty rigidity and stubborn complacency of the status quo." Gardner (1964, p. 48ff) ably describes the internal bonds from which the individual must escape. At Phase Three the individual, for the first time, takes his own authority seriously and his behavior is characterized by independence, creativity, self-confidence, and self-directedness.

Phase Three Consciousness. Rather than a world that is "given," a Phase Three consciousness perceives a world that is "created," a human project in which the self must participate. The individual finds meaning in and accepts responsibility for revitalizing, even reshaping, the environments in which he lives. In his concern for the quality of life and its renewal, the Phase Three person may focus his activity on guaranteeing the ecological balance of the natural environment, on ensuring human rights and justice in the social order, on improving the conditions for personal growth within his family or corporation. An individual in Phase Three is motivated by his personal need to express his creative insights, to be his own self, to direct his life, and to own his ideas and enterprises.

In the course of human development, the individual begins to move into a Phase Three consciousness when he no longer needs the affirmation of others to realize his self-worth and he no longer finds meaning in merely living up to the expectations of others. His sense of self-worth has become internalized; internal, personal expectations for himself replace external ones; the self begins to take charge. A personal sense of power and authority replaces institutional control or behavior. Consequently creativity and imagination are prized and a new-found sense of honesty makes conformity hypocritical. The transition into a Phase Three consciousness will probably not occur before early adulthood; it could occur any time during adulthood; or it may never occur at all.

The independence characteristic of Phase Three should not be equated with a radical disregard for the established order and the laws that govern it. Order and law are good, but law is to be critiqued and, when necessary, reformulated to meet the demands of justice. Phase Three persons expect authority to be adaptive and imaginative, responsive to changing conditions. However, a Phase Three person also respects the authority of his own inner voice, that internal urging which calls him to be true to himself rather than to be guided by external voices in society or by the majority opinion. Interestingly Ira Progoff does not see a contradiction between respect for law and order and a critical evaluation of it directed by the voice of an individual's conscience. In **The Symbolic and the Real** (1973) he describes Socrates' defense of himself before the Athenian court just prior to his final condemnation and death. In his defense Socrates

> described his intimate feeling of why it was important for him to live his life as he had been living it. It was not a question of intellectual philosophy, but of a calling that came to him from two sources, an outward source and an

inward source, which Socrates understood as ultimately not separate at all from one another. The outward source of his calling was the gods of the Greek Pantheon; and to this the Oracle at Delphi testified. The inward source of his calling was the oracle within himself. He described this as the "divine faculty of which the internal oracle is the source." To Socrates the inward and the outward were two aspects of a single principle. It was in the light of this unity that he could state his belief "that there were gods in a sense higher than any of my accusers' belief in them."

Internal authority should not be confused with lack of cooperation or with a radical independence in which one does not listen to another. Rather, it means that the individual must consciously assume responsibility for the final decision himself. Kohlberg's Level III, the post-conventional autonomous level, describes behavior in which the individual attempts to define the morality of an action apart from the authority of principles held by significant persons or groups. A person listens to the voice of law and order, but only after criticism and careful evaluation.

To actualize his own being, the self in Phase Three transcends its own limited world, becoming sensitive to the rights of all mankind. Liberation, freedom and independence become far more than matters for personal development. They become matters for group social action and national liberation. Thomas Jefferson clearly expressed this mentality over 200 years ago when it became necessary for "one people to dissolve the political bonds which connected them with another" because they held the belief that life, liberty, and the pursuit of happiness were inalienable rights. The Declaration of Independence illustrates a Phase Three consciousness.

Many contemporary examples of Phase Three behavior exist but to identify what may be the most obvious can cause a problem. On the one hand, there are outstanding individuals whose personal concern for critical social and political issues is followed by responsible action, often at great cost. On the other hand, social action and political protest movements attract a variety of followers whose motivation and behavioral expression are nothing more than immature fadism or adolescent revolt. Suffice it to say that the late sixties and early seventies had their share of both types. Clearly, serious concern for the rights of minorities—black, Latino, women; efforts to eliminate the causes of cultural poverty and institutional injustice; opposition to U.S. military intervention in Southeast Asia; active interest in conserving the sources of energy and preserving an ecological balance—all grow out of a Phase Three consciousness. So do a variety of less visible expressions involving an individual life-style of dedicated service, creative imagination, high pain-tolerance, empathy, and play where the person finds meaning in **being** oneself.

Phase Four Consciousness. At Phase Four the individual's perception of the world expands dramatically and enters the person's consciousness as a series of tasks to be performed in conjunction with other like-minded men and women. The individual self is transcended and the persons act interdependently with other selves. The "I" has become "we."

These like-minded persons see the world as a mystery, but one for which men and women must take authority by choosing to create and enhance the environment. That is to say, men and women take authority over creation and work in cooperation with others and with nature itself in a common interdependent action that seeks harmonious balance. Such persons view the world as an unfinished work, an incomplete opus. Its present condition is not nearly so important as its future potentiality. However, this viewpoint implies no disregard or lack of concern for existing persons or communities, for they too are viewed in their potentiality as much as in their actuality. In Phase Four the world is perceived as a mystery-to-be-cared-for.

The self is transcended not only as the individual "I" becomes a community "we" but also in the communal call to mankind to renew the face of the earth. In the common interdependent action, among men and women and with nature itself, a unity begins to emerge between mankind and his technology. As the human spirit transforms matter, the individual extends his physical and personal being into the external order in the technological process of building the earth. Eileen Cantin (1974), writing on Mounier, describes these two levels of transcendence.

> The most basic mode of transcendence and the one which paves the way for higher modes is production. By modifying the world around him and making it more and more an objectification of himself, the person extends his physical and, through it, his personal being. He gives himself a new and more extensive body and he gives something of his own humanity to impersonal reality. Transformation of matter implies not only its personalization, but also provides new opportunities for the emergence of the human spirit. As the condition of matter is transformed so are the conditions for the expression and the emergence

of the human spirit heightened . . .

The second level of transcendence is that which is achieved through interpersonal relations. The person is called to surpass himself by sharing himself with another person . . . A community of persons finds its cohesion within a We which is itself a Person. The We emerges from the community in much the same fashion as the I emerges from its material conditions, i.e., in response to a call.

The harmonious balance envisioned in Phase Four seeks to see things in their wholeness and to understand the interrelatedness of parts, frequently opposing parts, to each other and to the whole. Understood in terms of Newtonian physics, harmony is seen as a state of equilibrium that can be achieved if we recognize the order of the universe and the mathematical laws that govern it. This view is characteristic of Phase Two. Quantum physics, on the other hand, discounts the notion that reality is static, in a constant state of order and balance. Rather, it suggests that the opposite is the case. Understood in terms of quantum physics, harmony is seen in movement and tension, in the reconciliation of opposites. Congruence, or the suitable relatedness of things to each other

and of parts to the whole, is essential to a Phase Four understanding of harmony.

The concept of harmony applies to the inner life of the individual as well as to the external world. Insights from Eastern religions and from depth psychology have raised in the Western mind a new awareness of the potential for personal harmony. At Phase Four, intimacy and solitude become unitive. However, the Phase Four person realizes that this harmony must be extended to technology and society at large—the global community. Inner harmony must be integrated with social harmony through an appropriate technology. Ivan Illich's **Tools for Conviviality** (1973) suggests that man must be in control of his tools, of his technology, rather than be a victim of them. E. F. Schumacher's **Small Is Beautiful** (1973) suggests that we need to develop an intermediate technology that is congruent with the growth needs of the persons who use it. Convivial tools and intermediate technology both illustrate a Phase Four consciousness.

At Phase Four, then, the world is perceived as a mystery for which we, like-minded persons, must care. The world is perceived globally or holistically—the natural world, the human communities and persons who live in it, the technology that has transformed it. Within this global context, Phase Four selves seek to enliven, to nurture persons and communities from the context of consciousness that is meaningful to them. In doing so, the interdependent "we" responds to the common call to strive for global harmony, to build and to renew the face of the earth.

The Four Phases: A Summary. We have described the four phases of consciousness in terms of three elements: (1) how the world is perceived by the individual, (2) how the individual perceives its self to function within that world, and (3) what human needs the self seeks to satisfy. We have attempted to illustrate each phase so that it can be understood as an all-encompassing attitudinal framework within which the individual makes meaning out of his world and for himself and his behavior. Here, we look at the developmental aspect of these three aspects. Developmentally, the individual perceives his world as a **mystery** over which he has **no control,** a **problem** with which he can **cope,** then a **project** in which he must **participate,** and finally a **mystery** for which **we** must **care.** Initially the self **exists** at the center of a **hostile world,** then, **does things** to succeed and to belong in a **social world, acts** on the **created world** with conscience and independence and finally **selves give** life to the **global world.** At Phase One, the self seeks to satisfy the **physical needs** for food, pleasure/sex, warmth, and shelter, then the **social need** for **acceptance, affirmation, approval,** and **achievement.** At Phase Three the self seeks to satisfy the **personal need** to express **creative insights, be oneself, direct one's life,** and **own one's ideas and enterprises.** Finally, like-minded **selves** seek to satisfy the **communal need** for **global harmony** by nurturing persons and communities from their phase of consciousness. These developmental aspects of the four phases are illustrated in Figure 2.1 below.

The Stages of Value Development

The literature on value theory and motivation is extensive and for a more comprehensive explanation of values we refer the reader to it. Here we intend to relate values to a person's meaning system—his phase of consciousness—and his behavior—his level of skill development. We shall then illustrate the stages of value development as components of the phases of consciousness.

Values and Meaning. The values that operate in a person's life originate in his consciousness and are expressed in his behavior. Values give a person meaning and at the same time shape his life-style. They are human motivators. At a specific period in an individual's life, some values constitute the very core of meaning; at another period a different set of values form the center of his meaning system. These **primary** values change as the person matures. For example, in Phase One life is meaningful when the self is preserved, is secure, and finds delight. For someone in a Phase Two consciousness, self-preservation, security, and self-delight would not satisfy his quest for meaning. These have been replaced by other primary values—belonging, self-worth, self-competence. The primary values constituting the core of meaning at Phases One and Two bear a strong similarity to what Maslow (1968) calls D-cognition values. In his hierarchy of needs Maslow describes the basic physical needs and the belonging social-ego needs as being necessary for good mental health. At the same time, it appears that Maslow's self-actualizing values resemble the meaning system of persons in Phases Three and Four. These B-cognition values are essential to personal growth—self-actualization, service as vocation, human dignity, intimacy and solitude. Thus, values that give meaning to life and that motivate behavior change over time. These shifts seem to relate to the individual's phase of consciousness.

The Four Phases of Consciousness

Elements	Phase One	Phase Two	Phase Three	Phase Four
How the WORLD is perceived by the individual.	The world is a MYSTERY over which I have NO CONTROL.	The world is a PROBLEM with which I can COPE.	The world is a PROJECT in which I must PARTICIPATE.	The world is a MYSTERY for which WE must CARE.
How the individual perceives its SELF to FUNCTION in the world.	The self EXISTS at the center of a HOSTILE WORLD.	The self DOES things to succeed and to belong in a SOCIAL WORLD.	The self ACTS on the CREATED WORLD with conscience and independence.	Selves GIVE LIFE to the GLOBAL WORLD.
What HUMAN NEEDS the self seeks to satisfy.	The self seeks to satisfy the PHYSICAL NEED for food, pleasure, shelter.	The self seeks to satisfy the SOCIAL NEED for acceptance, affirmation, approval, achievement.	The self seeks to satisfy the PERSONAL NEED for being one's self, directing one's life, owning one's ideas.	Selves seek to satisfy the COMMUNAL NEED for global harmony.

Figure 2.1:—The developmental aspects of the four phases of consciousness.

Rokeach (1973) makes a useful distinction among types of values. He identifies instrumental values as those values desired not so much for themselves as for what they can lead to. Traditionally philosophers have called these **means** values. On the other hand, he speaks of terminal values, **ends** that are sought for their own sake. The primary values that constitute the core of meaning in a phase of consciousness parallel **ends** values.

Shifts in Consciousness. Movement from one phase of consciousness into another is dependent upon several factors. First, the individual's environment at his present phase must positively reinforce his personal effort to achieve primary values. In other words, at his present phase, he must have good experiences. He must enjoy the experience of security at Phase One, or at Phase Two, he must experience himself as belonging, worthwhile, competent. In the course of these positive experiences, the individual internalizes these values so that he consistently manifests behavior that expresses them.

48

His behavior indicates that a value has become actualized and incorporated into his meaning system. At this point he may become dissatisfied with his present world and begin to search for new sources of meaning—the next phase of consciousness. Finally, he needs to experience positive reinforcement from the environment of the phase to which he aspires.

At this point it is helpful to distinguish between values that center around personal activity and attitudes and those that focus outward toward institutions. With Rescher (1969) we recognize that values can be classified in numerous ways, but find that the individual-institutional distinction is useful in understanding the process of moving through a phase of consciousness. Individual values tend to focus on the person himself and can be expressed within a private sphere. Institutional values are defined from the point of view of the institution and therefore become manifest in a more public sphere. As an individual moves into a new phase of consciousness, the tendency is to acquire skill in the areas of the personal, more private, values first. Consequently, we have identified two stages within each phase of consciousness where the "A" Stage includes individual values and the "B" Stage includes institutional values. In Figure 2.2 below we have schematically illustrated **individual** and **institutional** values, **primary** and **means** values by taking examples from the two stages of value development in Phase Two.

As mentioned above, behavior is an indicator of the values on which a person operates. Values are never revealed in isolation, but rather in a group of several values ranked in a particular order. Moreover, there are different kinds of behavior through which a person expresses his values. For example, verbal behavior, which describes values, differs significantly from observed concrete behavior in which values are implicit. Of the latter, we can say that a value is actualized while, of the former, we only know that a value is aspired to. Between the past choices through which a value has been internalized and the future envisioned by value ideals, there exists the arena of the present in which conscious choice is exercised. Perhaps this point is best described as the cutting edge where the person is honing new behavior—acquiring skills—with all the awkwardness and confusion associated with periods of growth. In recognizing values in **act,** in **choice,** and in **vision,** we acknowledge not only the differences in strength the values possess, but also we receive some insight into the process of growth through the stages of value development. Some **means values** tend to be the **prime skill values** at each phase of consciousness. In Figure 2.3 we have summarized the eight stages of value development by indicating the **primary values** that constitute the individual's core of meaning and the **means values** that are the **prime skill values** enabling the individual to realize the core primary values. It can be noted that the primary values from Stage IA through IIB approximate Maslow's D-Values needed for good mental health, while the remaining primary values are similar to the B-Values essential to personal growth. For a complete list of primary and means values in each stage of development see Appendix A.

Phase Two Consciousness

ELEMENTS	
The World	The world is SOCIAL, an ESTABLISHED ORDER.
The Self	The self DOES things to BELONG and SUCCEED.
The Needs	The needs include ACCEPTANCE, AFFIRMATION, APPROVAL, ACHIEVEMENT.

STAGES OF VALUE DEVELOPMENT

	Stage II A INDIVIDUAL VALUES	Stage II B INSTITUTIONAL VALUES
PRIMARY VALUES Phase Two values which constitute core meaning and are ends in themselves.	Family/Belonging Self-worth	Self-competence/ Confidence
MEANS VALUES Some values related to		
BELONGING	Being Liked Social Affirmation Support—Peer	Membership Duty-Obligation Responsibility
The ESTABLISHED ORDER	Equilibrium Obedience/Duty Tradition	Law/Rule Loyalty/Respect Patriotism
SUCCESS	Function	Achievement/Success Education Productivity

Figure 2.2:—The two stages of value development in Phase Two illustrated by some characteristic values.

50

Primary and Means Values
in the Eight Stages of Value Development

	PHASE ONE		PHASE TWO		PHASE THREE		PHASE FOUR	
ELEMENTS IN THE PHASES OF CON-SCIOUSNESS	The self struggles to survive in an alien, oppressive, capricious environment.		The self seeks to belong in a significant human environment and to be approved by significant persons.		The self strives to re-shape the natural, social, and cultural environments with conscience and independence.		Selves enliven the global environment through the union of intimacy and solitude and the harmony of systems	
	Stage I A	Stage I B	Stage II A	Stage II B	Stage III A	Stage III B	Stage IV A	Stage IV B
PRIMARY VALUES which are **ends** in themselves and which constitute the **core of meaning.**	Self-preservation	Security	Family/ Belonging Self-worth	Self-compe-tence/ confidence	Life/ Self-actuali-zation Service/ Vocation	Being Self Human Dignity	Intimacy/ Solitude Trans-cendence	Ecority/ Beauty
MEANS VALUES which are **prime skill values.**	Safety/ Survival		Instrumen-tality Family Be-longing	Education	Empathy Health Indepen-dence	Account-ability/ Mutual Respon-sibility	Inter depend-dence	Convivial Tools/ Inter-mediate Techno-logy

Figure 2.3:—Primary and means values in the eight stages of value development.

Values and Skill Development. As we suggested in the discussion above, values originate in a person's consciousness—his meaning system—and are expressed in his behavior. When the individual consistently manifests behavior that is indicative of a value, he has actualized or internalized that value into his meaning system. In other words, he has learned new behavior—acquired skills—with which he consistently acts. Behavior, then, can be conceptually related to values in two ways: (1) behavior can be considered as a value indicator, and (2) behavior can be considered as a learned skill associated with the value it indicates. While we recognize that there are innumerable ways of categorizing skills and values, we have found it useful to look at values in terms of the four kinds of skills described in Chapter I: instrumental, interpersonal, imaginal, and system skills.

Figure 2.2 above can be used to illustrate values as skills. The Phase Two values associated with belonging—being liked, peer support, duty-obligation, responsibility—become internalized as the individual becomes skilled in interpersonal behaviors. Similarly, the values related to success— competence, achievement, education, productivity—are achieved as the instrumental skills that enable the individual to do a task are developed. Values as skills are more easily understood when they are considered in a specific context. It is the purpose of this book to consider values as skills within the context of organizational leadership.

In the following chapter, we examine organizational leadership within the framework of Hall's theory of consciousness and value development with special attention given to the skills acquired within each of the four phases. As a reference for Chapter III, we have listed the primary and means values according to the four skill categories and according to the stage at which they are developed. This information is found in Appendix B. However, we call attention to this analysis of values as skills here because it suggests that (1) imaginal skills develop in each phase of consciousness, and (2) the other skill categories tend to dominate one or two phases only. Appendix B illustrates that instrumental skills tend to dominate Phases One and Two; interpersonal skills, Phase Three; systems skills, Phase Four.

Chapter III

Toward Servant Leadership

Servant and Leader—can these two roles be fused in one real person, in all levels of status and calling? If so, can that person live and be productive in the real world of the present? My sense of the present leads me to say yes to both questions.
Robert Greenleaf (1977, p. 7)

Inspired by the vision of Robert Greenleaf, that in a single person the leader can also be servant, we began to explore the process of leadership development that ultimately results in the servant leadership role. Administrative theory as well as experience in management consulting have led us to believe that the development of organizational leadership can be understood in terms of consciousness and value development. Moreover, we are convinced that leadership styles can never

be separated from followership styles because both are directly related to the maturity, or level of psychological development, characteristic of the leader and of the led. However, as we observed leader-follower styles, it became evident that all the styles did not fit neatly into the four phases of consciousness. In addition to observing four leadership styles, each encompassed within its phase of consciousness, we observed what could be called transitional levels, that is, we watched individuals in leadership positions struggle with the awkward process of moving from one phase of consciousness to another. These three in-between levels seem to be real stages in the development of leadership potential, their significance lying in the fact that they presage either exceptional growth or serious regression.

Thus seven levels of leadership-followership emerged. Each level can be described in terms of the attitudes, values, and skills of both the leaders and the followers. The seven levels correspond to the process of value development in that they describe a hierarchy of skills. A leader or follower cannot function effectively at a later level unless he or she has acquired the basic skills of the earlier levels. An individual need not have experienced each level in a leadership position but he or she will have experienced each level as a follower. Chapter III describes the seven leader-followership styles and then explores the conditions and processes that enable individuals to move through these styles toward executive-level servant leadership.

Seven Leadership Followership Styles

Four leader-follower styles are easily associated with attitudes, values, and skills characteristic of persons whose world view is encompassed by a single phase of consciousness. Since we are convinced that leader-follower behavior mirror-image each other, we have identified each level with a label characterizing the persons who, as leaders or as followers, will behave in a predictable manner. For example, the alienated man who perceives his world as hostile—Phase One—will, as a leader, act autocratically, as a dictator or tyrant. However, if the alienated man is a follower, he will experience leadership as oppressive yet be totally dependent on it. Figure 3.1 labels the four levels of leader - followership, each encompassed within a single phase of consciousness.

54

THE CHARACTER OF MAN	PHASE	THE WORLD VIEW
The ALIENATED Man . . .	ONE	. . . in a HOSTILE world.
The ORGANIZATION Man . . .	TWO	. . . in a SOCIAL world.
The INDEPENDENT Man . . .	THREE	. . . in a world as PROJECT.
Man as PROPHET . . .	FOUR	. . . in a world to be CARED FOR.

Figure 3.1:—The character of man associated with the four levels of leadership, each of which is encompassed within a phase of consciousness.

However, in addition to these four levels, there appears to be a distinctive type of leader-follower behavior that characterizes persons whose vision aspires to a subsequent phase of consciousness, but whose behavior and skills are indicative of an earlier stage of value development. Although these might be called transitional levels, they contribute essential elements to the process of leadership development. In Figure 3.2, the transitional levels are related to the phases of consciousness that each one bridges. While still rooted in the alien world of Phase One, the preservative man maintains

THE CHARACTER OF MAN	TRANSITION PHASE	THE WORD VIEW
The PRESERVATIVE Man	ONE/TWO	. . . in a HOSTILE world.
The COMMUNAL Man	TWO/THREE	. . . in a SOCIAL world.
The CREATOR Man	THREE/FOUR	. . . in the world as PROJECT.

Figure 3.2:—The character of man associated with the three transitional levels of leadership.

things as they are given but tries to do it more humanely. The communal man, while still needing to belong to the established social order, begins to believe in his own authority and to take responsibility for the quality of his world. The creator man can exercise his own creativity and authority with conscience and independence and begins to share the vision of those persons who see the world as a mystery to be cared for. As Figure 3.3 suggests, the preservative man's behavior reflects values and skills associated with Stages I-B and II-A; communal man bridges Stage II-B and III-A; creator man III-B and IV-A.

THE CHARACTER OF MAN WITHIN PHASES	VALUE STAGES		THE CHARACTER OF MAN BETWEEN PHASES	
(1) The ALIENATED Man	I			
		B A	The PRESERVATIVE Man	(2)
(3) The ORGANIZATION Man	II			
		B A	The COMMUNAL Man	(4)
(5) The INDEPENDENT Man	III			
		B A	The CREATOR Man	(6)
(7) Man as PROPHET	IV			

Figure 3.3:—The seven levels of leadership related to the stages of value development and phases of consciousness.

Level 1: The Alienated Man. Alienated man exercises the most primitive style of leadership. In a lonely, hostile world, with an enemy "out there," to be an autocratic dictator or tyrant is to live a reasonable life-style. In time of war, when there is an enemy "out there," it would be disastrous for military leadership not to exercise this pattern of behavior. In less actually alien circumstances, Level 1 corresponds to the organizational leader who operates out of McGregor's theory X assumption that people hate to work and must be threatened with punishment if they are to work toward organizational objectives. Robert Townsend (1972, p. 77) with tongue-in-cheek, describes a Level 1 executive officer:

> The best two guarantees that the chief executive officer will work full time are hunger and fear. He has to hunger for the company to succeed; and he has to have so much of his own money tied up in the company that fear of failure is constantly with him.

Fear and hunger describe both the leader and follower at Level 1.

At Level 1 the followers perceive themselves as victims of power—a dictatorial state, the magic of the witch-doctor, the strength of an inhumane boss. Distance between leader and follower increases alienation and dependency. Hall recalls visiting a monastery where even the religious art reflected both distance and dependency between the monks and their abbot.

> Coming down a long staircase, I was confronted by a huge mural of Christ on a flat wall some forty feet high. He was simply standing with welcoming arms. I was startled by the face, so I turned to the guide and said, "Excuse me, but the face in the mural seems familiar." "Yes," he responded, "you

are observant, it is the face of the Father Superior of this house!"

At Level 1 the leadership style is autocratic, the followers are dependent and oppressed. For leader and follower alike, the world is hostile and the individual must struggle to survive.

Level 2: The Preservative Man. For the preservative man survival is still paramount, but the world is not quite so alien. He can cope, just cope; but basically he feels overwhelmed. The style is common: the president of a small company who acts like a father to a family; the teacher who possesses the "truth" that is passed on to the student; the successful politician who employs his family and friends. In Level 2 the dictator has become benevolent, even paternal, in his behavior. Raymond Brown (1970) points out that early in Hebrew history priestly functions were actively carried out by patriarchs who acted as the head of the family tribe.

Studs Terkel (1972, p. 77) quotes a business consultant who describes the corporation as a jungle. "You're thrown in on your own and you're constantly battling to survive. When you learn to survive, the game is to become the conqueror, the leader." Clearly the world remains alien, but the challenge is to "conquer." The leader is less overwhelmed; he can cope with, but not change, his world. His vision is to preserve himself and his world. In another place Terkel (1972, p. 397) describes a conflict characteristic of a Level 2 factory owner who reflects on his relationship with his workers.

> So I have to show a profit, that's the name of the game. I have been working here 27 or 28 years. I feel I owe them something. I don't know how to compensate them. At least if I go public, I can offer them stocks. I'd like to repay people. This is a way of saying thank you. I never tell people I'm the boss. I get red and flustered. I'm ashamed of it. When they find out—frankly speaking, people are parasites. A man comes in and I'm working like a worker, he tells me everything, he talks from the bottom of his heart. The minute he finds out you're in charge, he looks up to you. Actually, he hates you.

The boss betrays his ambivalence. At one moment, he is benevolent, paternal; at the next moment, "people are parasites" who hate him.

Followers in Level 2 remain dependent personalities who experience leaders somewhat more positively than at Level 1. The follower blindly obeys and is servant to a variety of leader symbols—the wise old man, the caring father, at times, "the

Godfather," or fairy godmother. Such behavior makes meaning for the person whose life bridges Phases One and Two consciousness.

Level 3: The Organization Man. Autocracy continues into Level 3 as the leadership style but with a significant shift. The organization man, leader and follower, is loyally devoted to the institution, to the bureaucracy. Competence and productivity are valued but always within the "system." Even Bell Telephone, which basically connects two individuals with each other, advertises on national TV with a jigsaw puzzle coming together of its own accord accompanied by the caption—"Remember—System is better." The organization man retains one foot firmly planted in Stage II A with its emphasis on belonging associated with the family. Although a bureaucrat, he may also be seen as a benevolent paternalist. He listens to followers but supports ideas only if they reflect deep loyalty to the organization.

William Whyte (1957, pp. 3–4) suggests that the organization man has penetrated almost every field in our society.

> The corporation man is the most conspicuous example, but he is only one; for the collectivization so visible in the corporation has affected almost every field of work. Blood brother to the business trainee off to join duPont is the seminary student who will end up in the church hierarchy, the doctor headed for the corporate clinic, the physics Ph.D. in a government laboratory, the intellectual on the foundation-sponsored team project, the engineer graduate in the huge drafting room at Lockheed, the young apprentice in a Wall Street law factory. They are all, as they so often put it, in the same boat.

"Being in the same boat" suggests that in each case the individual is subsumed into the institution; the person becomes a cog in the bureaucratic wheel.

Drucker (1967, p. 78), on the other hand, relates an anecdote about Robert E. Lee that illustrates a view of his military organization where individual performance, getting the job done, took precedence over a smoothly operating system," both highly valued in Level 3.

> One of his generals, the story goes, had disregarded orders and had thereby completely upset Lee's plan—and not for the first time, either. Lee, who normally controlled his temper, blew up in a towering rage. When he had simmered down, one of his aides asked respectfully, "Why

don't you relieve him of his command?" Lee, it is said, turned around in complete amazement, looked at the aide, and said, "What an absurb question. He performs!"

Today, high performance and efficiency characterize both the Level 3 leader and follower and with Ma Bell both remember that the "System is better."

Level 4: The Communal Man. Persons in Level 4 are struggling to bridge the gap between a Phase Two and Phase Three consciousness and the conflict creates confusion between the roles of leader and follower. The leadership style is laissez-faire with the person in the leader position assuming the role of clarifier, supporter, and listener. Likewise the follower also clarifies, supports, and listens. Consequently, nothing gets done. Actually, laissez-faire leadership is probably a misnomer as Seifert and Clinebell (1974, p. 143) suggest.

> The laissez-faire leader does exert some influence, as does any member in a group situation, but his action style keeps that influence minimal. He may hold a leadership title, but he does not play the role.

Clinebell goes on to note that such a style is self-defeating. In fact, the passivity of the leader "stimulates anger in the group by defeating their expectations." Level 4 leadership is usually short-lived unless the leader's role is to facilitate a sensitivity group. Level 4 leaders quickly move to a democratic, but decisive style, characteristic of Level 5 or they regress to Levels 1 or 2.

Level 5: The Independent Man. At Level 5 leaders and followers have begun to experience fully their own creativity and authority. Consequently, followership becomes poor participation. The leader is democratic, but for the first time the person who leads experiences his own initiative and power. He is entrepreneurial beyond survival and security; his self-directedness considers the world as a place of invention. Traditionally this charisma was seen as the property of aristocrats or exceptional personalities—the "great man" theory of leadership. We feel that Max Weber's notion of charismatic leadership accurately describes Level 5 leaders.

> Unquestionably, many western social scientists have been influenced by the Weberian idea of the leader who enjoys his authority not through enacted position or traditional dignity, but owing to gifts of grace—charisma—by virtue of which he is set apart from other men. (Tucker, 1968, p. 731)

To this description, Tucker adds that the charismatic leader is "treated as endowed with supernatural, superhuman or, at least, specifically exceptional powers or qualities." With this statement we do not agree, for it is our conviction that charisma is developmental and personally available to all. We believe it is attested to in much modern behavioral science literature, for example: Maslows self-actualized man, Erikson's integral man, and Jung's individuated man. We believe that Level 5 is the minimal requirement for corporate leadership today.

The Level 5 leader is enthusiastic, visionary; he possesses the skills of empathy and confrontation. He listens attentively and with care. He takes peer authority seriously. He wants to bring others' comments to bear on his decisions, but he may be so independent that he often fails to do so. He aspires to be truly democratic, but fails to put time aside to build the kind of administrative team or community that allows his democracy to work. The style is genuinely facilitative and democratic, when the leader is available! The Level 5 leader may be the school superintendent who is so creatively busy that he always arrives halfway through a planning meeting or

the local executive director, so needed by the executive council in New York or London, that frequently he is not at home directing his own organization.

Level 6: The Creator Man. Level 6 marks the apex in leadership capability. For creator man, leadership is always plural. Based on the resources of interdependent peers, the Level 6 executive creates a corporate community among his closest administrators. Interdependent administrators participate collegially in a genuinely democratic operation. Leadership at this level can differentiate between situations that demand the use of interpersonal skills from circumstances that require the use of systems skills. Both interpersonal and systems skills are highly developed in Level 6 leaders.

Level 6 also marks the transition into a new phase of consciousness in which the individuals always view the parts in relation to the whole. Their global vision penetrates and alters the local corporation and its administrative style. Leadership, then, concerns itself not only with the efficiency and productivity of the corporation, but also with the quality of human interaction within the organizations and the good of the society as a whole. The system must be efficient but it must also reinforce individual human or spiritual development within its members and within the larger society.

For individuals at Level 6 the predominant values are presence, interdependence, and harmony. Perhaps it is a quality of extraordinary presence that enables us to identify the Level 6 person in his servant-leader role. Robert Greenleaf (1977, p. 7) himself a great leader, has written superbly on the leader as servant, an idea that came from his reading of Herman Hesse.

In this story, we see a band of men on a mythical journey, probably also Hesse's own journey. The central figure of the story is Leo, who accompanies the party as the servant who does their menial chores, but who sustains them with his spirit and his song. He is a person of extraordinary presence. All goes well until Leo disappears. Then the group falls into disarray, and the journey is abandoned. They cannot make it without the servant, Leo. The narrator, one of the party, after some years of wandering, finds Leo and is taken into the Order that had sponsored the journey. There he discovers that Leo, whom he had first known as servant, was, in fact, the titular head of the Order, its guiding spirit, a great and noble leader.

The leader as servant is sustained by the vision created by the prophets of our times who provide us with clues to how global harmony might be achieved.

Level 7: Man as Prophet. Level 7 is not to be found in the practical order of leadership. Rather, it is the vision that gives perspective to six levels of leadership described above. The Level 7 leader exists only as a voice, as a prophet who enables leadership at all levels to become aware of the larger, sounder global vision. It is the voice that relates local women's rights to overpopulation in India to the need for a better masculine/feminine balance in all persons. It is the voice that relates the oil crisis to overproduction of food in the United States to global interdependence as a value we all need. It is the voice that points to interdependence as the essential value at every level of administration in every institution. It is the voice that claims that world peace and global cooperation on natural resources will be achieved only as these values are internalized locally.

Robert Greenleaf (1977, p. 9) recognizes the need for leaders to listen carefully to these prophetic voices.

> I am hopeful for these times, despite the tension and conflict, because more natural servants are trying to see clearly the world as it is and are listening carefully to prophetic voices that are speaking **now.**

> They are challenging the pervasive injustice with greater force, and they are taking sharper issue with the wide disparity between the quality of society they know as reasonable and possible with available resources, and on the other hand, the actual performance of the whole range of institutions that exist to serve society.

The vision that Level 7 upholds deals with societal harmony that flows from a personal meaning system found in that kind of intimacy and solitude usually thought of as deeply religious—namely, the union that comes from the higher stages of contemplation. The skills associated with the values of harmony and the union of intimacy and solitude include such ascetical practices as passive concentration in prayer. They also include the skills involved in the ability to sustain a deep level of interpersonal intimacy such as is possible after years of marriage between husband and wife. James Fowler posits this realm of experience as his sixth stage of faith and describes it as follows.

62

Conflicts and paradox are embraced as essential to the integrity of Being, but are unified in a no longer paradoxical grasp of the oneness of Being . . . Stage Six has the ability to respond to and feel commonality with the concreteness and individuality of persons while also relating to and evoking their potential . . . Active compassion for a commonwealth of being is expressed including but transcending group differences and conflicts. (Hennessy, 1976, p. 202)

Leadership/Followership Styles: A Summary. Our experience suggests that seven levels of leadership and followership styles can be identified which relate directly to the four phases of consciousness and eight stages of value development. As leaders, persons whose world view is limited by the first two phases of consciousness will behave as autocrats—Levels 1–3. At Level 4 leadership is laissez-faire, but cannot sustain this style indefinitely. The leader quickly develops the skills of democratic leadership characteristic of Levels 5 and 6 or returns to an autocratic style of an earlier level. Democratic leadership occurs only when the leader has internalized the values and developed the skills associated with the third phase of consciousness. Figure 3.4 below schematically summarizes the seven levels of leadership and followership styles and relates them to the phases of consciousness and the stages of value development. Appendix C illustrates more fully the seven levels of leadership in relation to consciousness and value development.

Developing Leadership: Consciousness and Value Theory Revisited

The levels of leadership parallel the phases of consciousness and the stages of value development not only in their content but also in the processes of moving from a lower to a higher level. Therefore, we pause briefly to recall four aspects of Hall's consciousness and value theory that bear directly on the development of leadership. (1) The experience of leadership styles is developmental in nature. (2) A shift in consciousness precedes the movement from one level to a subsequent level. (3) New values become actualized through the development of skills. (4) The four types of skills— imaginal, instrumental, interpersonal, and systems skills—tend to develop at specific phases of consciousness.

The Seven Levels of Leadership

LEADERSHIP	LEVEL 1	LEVEL 2	LEVEL 3	LEVEL 4	LEVEL 5	LEVEL 6	LEVEL 7
STYLE OF LEADERSHIP	AUTOCRAT as Tyrant Dictator	AUTOCRAT as Godfather Benevolent dictator	AUTOCRAT as Bureaucrat Benevolent paternalist	LAISSEZ FAIRE LEADER as Clarifier Supporter Listener	DEMOCRAT as Charismatic leader Facilitator Producer/ Creator	DEMOCRAT as Collegial leader Servant interdependent administrators	VISIONARIES as Liberators Synergists Global Network of Persons
THE CHARACTER OF MAN	THE ALIENATED MAN	THE PRESERVATIVE MAN	THE ORGANIZA-TIONAL MAN	THE COMMUNAL MAN	THE INDEPENDENT MAN	THE CREATOR MAN	THE MAN as PROPHET
STYLE OF FOLLOWER-SHIP	Oppressed Totally dependent	The Servant Blindly obedient	The Dedicated servant Loyally devoted to Institution	Role Confusion Clarifier Supporter Listener	Intermediate peer participation	Collegial participation	Peer visionaries
FOLLOWER-SHIP	LEVEL 1	LEVEL 2	LEVEL 3	LEVEL 4	LEVEL 5	LEVEL 6	LEVEL 7

VALUES	Stage I A	Stage I B	Stage II A	Stage II B	Stage III A	Stage III B	Stage IV A	Stage IV B
CONSCIOUS NESS	PHASE ONE		PHASE TWO		PHASE THREE		PHASE FOUR	

Figure 3.4:—The seven levels of leadership within the phases of consciousness and the stages of value development.

When we say that the experience of leadership is developmental we mean that the levels are sequential and probably irreversible. That is to say, good experiences of leadership at earlier levels, even when experienced in the role of follower, provide the basis for successfully moving into subsequent levels. Bad experiences of earlier leadership levels may thwart, even prevent, growth into a later level. Although the levels of development are sequential, environmental circumstances may force a leader who possesses skills of a later level to return to an earlier level. It should be noted that, although the experience of leadership is developmental, an individual leader need not experience each level in the role of leader. For example, an executive capable of democratic

64

leadership—Level 5—need not have been an autocratic leader personally—Levels 1 or 2 —but, as a follower, he or she will have experienced autocratic leadership at some time in life.

Values that are initially future ideals become part of his present behavior as the individual begins to make choices based on them. They become internalized as the person develops the skills enabling him to act comfortably and to accept comfortably the consequences of his choices. When the new values become actualized in leadership behavior the individual has moved to a new level of leadership style.

The four types of skills—imaginal, instrumental, interpersonal, and systems skills—tend to develop at specific phases of consciousness. Consequently, we can expect that the seven leadership styles can be described in terms of the types of skills associated with the values and consciousness of the persons in the leader role. But of greater importance than a description of leadership styles is the fact that an understanding of the consciousness-value-skill development process enables us to create conditions for the development of new leadership styles that more closely approximate the prophetic vision voiced by the men of ideas in Level 7 and incarnated by the servant leaders of Level 6. We turn now to an exploration of the processes and conditions in which individuals can move toward servant leadership at the executive level of organizations.

We shall examine the first three levels in which leadership is basically autocratic with the intention of identifying the good experiences at each level that lay the foundation for the future development of essential leader skills. We shall also look at the consciousness-value-skill processes that enable an individual to move through these levels. Then we shall turn our attention to Level 4—laissez-faire leadership and finally, to the democratic styles of Levels 5 and 6 where the roles of leader and servant merge.

The Leader as Autocrat: Levels 1, 2, and 3. The alienated man, as a leader, is a tyrant who dictates to his followers who in turn are oppressed and totally dependent. Both leader and follower fight to survive in their hostile worlds. For an adult, the experience is bound to be loathsome; but for the infant, it is bound to be the experience of life. The experience of Level 1 leadership teaches the skills of survival, and positive survival skills are essential to integrated leadership at the highest levels.

To be an absolutely obedient follower is a necessary learning experience. Level 1 marks the emergence of instrumental skills many of which are learned obediently and in total dependence on the teacher. In their early stages, the skills of reading, writing, and computing demand complete conformity. Other positive survival skills are developed—adaptability to change, high pain tolerance, risk and commitment. These skills, initiated at Level 1 but essential to Levels 6 and 7, may be underdeveloped in persons who are products of an affluent society.

However, the experience of survival, whether in childhood or in war, can lead persons to form negative skills. Self-preservation skills learned during a period of an actually alien environment may produce a state of person isolation that persists even when the actual world is no longer alien. This condition is mentally unhealthy. Domination becomes a way of avoiding personal loneliness rather than a way of leading. Helmuth Kaiser (1965, p. 77) claims that

> what distinguishes the leader from the domineering person is . . . the latter's preoccupation with power over others against the leader's preoccupation with what he plans to achieve by means of his power.

Tyrants are neurotic unless they really live in a hostile environment. Mental ill-health is the internalization of maladaptive skills—skills that might have been appropriate at another time but which have become disfunctional.

At Level 2 the world is not so alien. The leader, although still a dictator, is benevolent, even paternal. Followers, although dependent personalities, experience leadership somewhat more positively. As a transition between Phase One and Phase Two consciousness, Level 2 leadership style is confusing. The leader will listen to suggestions and concerns, but will, for the most part, only incorporate them in as the decision process if he feels they are his own ideas that he will dictate. Followers are expected to be blindly obedient but now they tend to believe in what they are told to do. When a follower breaks his or her relationship with the leader, the action is seen as personal treachery. The servant has betrayed his master—a notion that reflects the "godfather" dimension. To leave the family is a grave sin.

The Level 2 leader-follower relationship resembles that of parent to child. The leader can be a good parent or a bad parent. The instrumental skills that emerged in Level 1 are further developed making operational the newly envisioned values of family security and belonging. Care and love are often instrumental, especially when "doing" takes the form of providing for one's family. For a leader in a corporate setting,

66

to be a nurturing parent means to be a good teacher. For the follower, it means being a good learner. To learn rapidly from one's experience is a skill acquired by the leader that he encourages in his followers. If this skill is not developed, higher leadership capacity becomes impossible. Other technical or instrumental skills are learned from a nurturing parent—the ability to listen, to admit one's lack of knowledge, to seek understanding, to be obedient, to serve. Good experience of "parental" authority becomes the basis for one's own sense of personal authority in the future. It is also the basis for healthy attitudes toward social tradition, law and order.

It is equally important to avoid bad experiences of "parental" authority. The rigid "parent" becomes the overcontrolling leader with a scrupulous, legalistic orientation. In schools this occurs when teachers are more conscious of rules and grades than of persons and learning. Rigid persons need to preserve the status quo. Change is a threat because the past is known and therefore more secure. The rigid leader sees conflict and failure as a personal affront. Unfortunately, Level 2 leaders confuse work with family. They demand unreal levels of intimacy and sharing on the job. Inevitably these relationships break down, turning an administration into

emotional chaos. The inability to keep work and play relationships separate at this level returns as a serious problem at a later level.

Autocratic leadership continues at Level 3. In a leadership position, the organization man is the bureaucratic manager; as a follower, he is the dedicated servant loyally devoted to the institution. The leader is an organizational executive who stresses competent administration and management. Although still overshadowed by the image of the benevolent paternalist, the Level 3 leader shifts his focus from the care and nurture of his employees to the care and nurture of the organization itself. Since Level 3 leadership corresponds to Phase Two consciousness, it is not surprising to observe Stages II A and B values in administrative behavior. In examining the list of values found in Appendix A, the sense of benevolent paternalism becomes obvious. Stage II A values like family/belonging, being liked, and peer support are mixed with courtesy, duty and obligation. The sense of organization becomes evident in the Stage II B values of administration, membership/institution, rule/accountability that are mixed with self-confidence/competence, loyalty/respect, and workmanship/craft.

The organization executive who is also a benevolent paternalist demands loyalty not to himself, as in the previous style, but to the organization. He is goal conscious, concerned with efficiency, but genuinely kind. He listens to, even supports ideas, provided they reflect deep loyalty to the institution. However, "he" or "she" may disregard the ideas or information, because at Level 3, the leader is always singular and has the final word.

At Level 3 institutional authority has replaced "parental" authority. Good experiences of institutional authority are necessary for future leadership development. The well-run, administratively efficient organization instills loyalty and rewards work well done. Very bad experience within rigid institutions and the misuse of corporate authority can produce devastating consequences within individuals from which they may never recover. For some individuals, negative experiences of dependence in large systems such as government agencies or the Roman Catholic Church have disenabled their creative potential, preventing them from becoming self-initiating persons.

The instrumental skills associated with leadership, which emerged during the previous levels, are highly developed at Level 3. Success in corporate management depends on proficiency in such technical skills as communications, data processing, bookkeeping, and marketing. But all of these skills depend, to varying degrees, on human interaction. While scientific management stresses instrumentality, historically it was the two-dimensional theorists who recognized that for the organization to flourish, it must develop interpersonal interaction at more complex and creative levels. It is the good experience of corporateness that reinforces the emergence of interpersonal skills. McGregor (1973, p. 19) puts it this way:

> Among the characteristics essential for leadership are skills and attitudes which can be acquired or modified extensively through learning. These include competence in planning and initiating action, in problem solving, in keeping communication channels open and functioning effectively, in accepting responsibilities, and in the skills of social interaction. Such skills are not inherited, nor, in their acquisition, dependent on the possession of any unique pattern of inborn characteristics.

McGregor's point claims that interpersonal skills are learned. It is our point that they are learned through the good experience of organizational management. Among these skills we would include the ability to cope with conflict, to remain calm in high-stress situations, to articulate personal goals, to identify one's own feelings accurately, to share emotion quickly and creatively, to state anger objectively.

Autocratic Leadership: A Summary. Good experiences of the three levels of autocratic leadership provide the basis for the development of skills at the higher levels. From abrasively autocratic leaders an individual learns to develop positive survival skills such as adaptability to change, high pain tolerance, risk and commitment. From the "parent-teacher" leader comes the basis for one's own pesonal authority and the ability to learn quickly from one's experience. Through the experience of both, instrumental skills are learned that function effectively at the third level. From the experience of an efficiently administered organization, individuals begin to recognize the need for more creative forms of human interaction. The envisioned values of Phase II (Figure 2.2 above)—family and belonging, self-worth, competence and confidence—assume priority in administrative decisions and become internalized with the development of interpersonal skills in a corporate context. Instrumental skills that emerge at Levels 1 and 2 are proficient at Level 3. The need for improved interpersonal skills emerges at Level 3. The three levels of autocratic leadership styles span the first two phases of consciousness, (Figure 3.4 above), which are distinguished from the next phases of consciousness in that authority in Phases One and Two is always external to the individual. In other words, the individual "adapts" to his environment; he accepts, conforms, seeks external approval, relies on the direction of others. The transition to Phase Three, where authority is internal to the individual, where the individual exercises critical choice, is extremely awkward. Laissez-faire leadership is the style adopted by those persons whose vision has begun to include Phase Three values but who have yet to internalize them into actualized skills. Understandably, Level 4 leadership suffers from both confusion and awkwardness.

Laissez-faire Leadership Style: Level 4. At Level 4 the leader has grown dissatisfied with his role as "organization man" and strives to become a person guided by his own sense of creativity and authority. But he is caught between loyalty to his institution and his growing sense of independence. As illustrated in Appendix A, he acts out of the values characteristic of Stage II B and aspires to the values of Stage III A. On the one hand, his priorities include an emphasis on institutional values of Stage II B—administration/control, economics/success, membership/institution, productivity, rule/accountability. On the other hand, he experiences the need for new individual values of Stage III A—self-actualization, service/vocation, adaptability/flexibility, emphathy, equality/rights, and independence—most of which are interpersonal. The person feels a lingering allegiance to his friends and institutions—those secure arenas of belonging such as clubs and fraternities, but he longs to assert his independence, to experience the power of his own creativity, to be more "oneself," to share more intimately.

Caught between "belonging" and "being me," communal man often confuses relationships among his work associates with a need to share intimately among friends. When this happens and if, among the work group, interpersonal skills are not well-developed, anxiety, distress, and frustration often occur within an organization. However, this very notion—that institutional efficiency can be combined with personal intimacy and sharing—enters consciousness for the first time, providing a vision of what cooperation could mean in a corporate context. When an "organization man" becomes self-directed and shares deeply, a new vision of what institutions could be begins to emerge. It is the foundation of a Phase Four vision.

At Level 4 the roles of leader and of follower become confused and are replaced by the concept of "peer." When this occurs, it is typical for no one to lead, a situation that becomes destructive if not transcended quickly. The leader clarifies and supports but never confronts or makes a decision. The Level 4 leader maintains individuals and the institution; he entertains new ideas; but he never initiates new projects. Persons who have had bad experiences of corporateness or harsh institutional leadership tend to remain at this level. Their potential never comes to fruition. In a short time the administrative style of the organization has regressed to Level 1 or 2. The organizational environment has become oppressive. However, there is a positive side to the role confusion at Level 4. A new consciousness—that all leadership is plural—has emerged. This notion is essential to Levels 5 and 6. But it is necessary that the peer group develop interpersonal skills informed by a sense of personal authority and creativity. When the peer group develops the skills of empathy, group facilitation, value and goal clarification, it can function with strength and efficiency.

Level 4 leadership marks the transition of the leader from Phase Two to Phase Three. It is short-lived because the leader either moves into Level 5 by developing new interpersonal skills or he regresses to an earlier level, probably Level 2. In our experience we have seen executives in large corporations who failed to deepen their interpersonal skills become more paternal or maternal and overly critical of their subordinates. Often the executive has made a conscious choice not to grow. To involve oneself more interpersonally is threatening and difficult for individuals who are unaccustomed to expressing feeling rather than ideas. The move into Level 5 requires that authority be earned in the light of each new experience, whereas previously it has been given by virtue of position.

Some circumstances tend to mitigate against an individual's moving into Level 5. For example, large foundations in the United States, charged with giving away enormous sums of money each year to the public sector, often fall prey to the pressures and experiences of being "givers." By the nature of his task, the executive is placed in the role of "giver" or "parent." Some leave their positions after a year or so, feeling that they have become inauthentic. This probably means that they could not remain adults in a system that insisted that they be parents, treating their clients as children rather than equals. Unfortunately, clients reinforce this relationship when, in fact, they do perceive themselves as less than equal. Foundation executives who remain in their positions become more paternal and distant from their clients unless their interpersonal skills develop significantly. The problem of confusing parenting with leading becomes evident whenever one party is seen as the primary giver, such as giving aid to Third World nations or administering welfare programs. Only when the "giver" has developed his interpersonal skills can he enable both parties to recognize their mutual equalities. Giving aid is more than a simple economic transaction.

These examples suggest that for leadership to develop beyond Level 4, new interpersonal skills must be acquired. Level 4 provides the vision of leadership as plural; the vision of what institutions could be—efficient and caring. But unless interpersonal skills are deepened, the leadership style regresses quickly. To facilitate the transition into Phase Three consciousness—Level 5 leadership—we now consider an emerging awareness that values the imagination and use of a professional peer support structure.

Imagination and Interpersonal Skills. We recall from our discussion in Chapter 1 (p. 30) that imagination is the synergistic interaction of one's fantasy, emotions, and reflective intellect. The psychic energy used by the fantasy to convert data received into images, the emotions that evaluate the images created by the fantasy, and the reflective intellect that constructs ideas from the images—all reside deep within the

person. These processes are internal and unique to the individual. While imagination first emerges during infancy, it functions in various ways across the entire life-span. Imagination always plays a part in the development and use of instrumental and interpersonal skills.

However, most instrumental skills and many interpersonal skills are developed in Phases One and Two where a person's worth, competence, and confidence are measured by persons or authority that are external to the individual. Consequently, during these two phases, the unique personal contribution made in an internal world by the imagination cannot be taken too seriously. Imagination is discounted.

With the vision of Phase Three, however, imagination and its value break into consciousness in a new way. As the individual seeks to be "oneself," senses his own authority, and asserts his independence, he recognizes and values his imagination as being uniquely his own; he begins to take seriously his own creativity. Imagination, while operative during Phases One and Two, takes on a new role as the individual aspires to Stage III A values, many of which are interpersonal. Self-actualization, adaptability/flexibility, empathy, and equality become internalized as the individual seriously uses his imagination to synthesize new, complex data, to initiate totally new ideas from seemingly unrelated data, to learn from one's own experience. Since fantasy and feeling never function in isolation, the interpersonal skills that emerged in Level 3 develop more deeply, especially in the ability to identify one's own feelings accurately, to share emotion quickly and creatively, and to state anger objectively.

Professional Peer Support. For the most part institutional life does not reinforce growth beyond Level 3. Rather, individual leaders must become self-generating persons on their own initiative. Occasionally, laissez-faire leadership style is a screen for actual incompetence or for a feeling of inadequacy. The more alternatives that confront the leader, the greater must be his skill to deal with them. When a person is promoted beyond his skill competence, he or she becomes overwhelmed, chronically anxious, and paralyzed. Carried to an extreme, the leader suffers deep depression, even meaninglessness. This psychological state should not be confused with Level 4 laissez-faire leadership. The latter is a passing style; the former, a chronic problem, often leading to such problems as alcoholism or office promiscuity.

To avoid these problems and to enable the leader in Level 4 to move through it rapidly, the person needs to structure peer support groups. Sound corporation planning will build these groups into a leadership-training program for individuals at this level. At Level 4 the pressures of the administrative position increase at the same time that the individual administrator experiences a need for greater intimacy and sharing. A serious problem arises when the individual is unable to separate the needs of his work group from the needs of his family or intimacy group from his own needs to develop new interpersonal leadership skills. At Level 2, there is little differentiation between workers and family. For the paternal leader, we are all "family." The distinction is much clearer at Level 3. For the organization man, his work life is at the office; his family life is at home. Employees are not family. However, for the communal man at Level 4, family, friends, and fellow workers tend to become confused again, especially as the person becomes more intimate in all his or her relationships. Peer support groups can help the individual separate out the demands made by the various groups of which he is a member.

The peer group consists of persons who are professional equals but outside both the organization and the family. As an individual, a peer acts as friend and consultant to one's total experience, a third-party observer to both work and family. At the higher echelons of leadership, the person experiences greater pressure; the data are more complex; his or her personal life is more intimate. These factors create high maintenance needs at home and at work. The professional peer network provides the company executive or university president with personal support and with the awareness that leadership is in fact, plural, a cooperative venture.

David Richards, a bishop in the Episcopal Church, has researched and developed peer consultation with executives for a number of years. He writes:

Planned role-reversing—consulting dyads of peers—offers a type of supportive interaction. It is worth consideration because of the easy access it provides to the securing of professional help with one's task and the very low—even nonexistent—monetary cost that is involved. It personifies a statement made many years ago by Professor Biss in his introduction to **The Imitation of Christ.**

Men are bound together in this world in very singular ways . . . Life is so constituted we need reservoirs of every kind of excellence; of intelligence, of knowledge, of practical ability, of morality. No man is sufficient for himself. At every turn, he must borrow and he must lend.

74

Peer dyadic consultation is a process of borrowing and lending. From this process of interchange of ideas, abilities, knowledge, conceptualizing skills and workable schemes comes a mutual enrichment which enables both parties to face their respective tasks with increased enthusiasm, optimism and confidence. (Caplan and Killilea, 1976, p. 270)

Laissez-faire Leadership: A Summary. Laissez-faire leadership is a transitional style for the person who has become dissatisfied with the bureaucratic behavior of the organization man but has yet to develop fully the skills demanded by the democratic style of the independent man. As a style, it is short-lived; the leader moves on to Level 5 or regresses to Level 1 or 2. A good experience at Level 4 provides the person with two visions about future organizational leadership: (1) institutions can be both efficient and caring, and (2) leadership, at its highest level, is always plural. A person moves through Level 4 more quickly by recognizing the place of imagination and by consciously valuing its contribution to the development of personal authority and interpersonal skills. Professional peers facilitate the process of separating the demands made by one's associates at work and one's family at home by becoming a third party/friend-observer to the leader's total experience. As the individual's sense of independence grows, as personal authority and creativity are taken seriously, as interpersonal skills develop more deeply, the person moves into the third phase of consciousness and, as a leader, begins to function in a truly democratic style.

Toward Servant Leadership: Levels 5 and 6. Having moved fully into Phase Three consciousness, the independent man savors his newly acquired sense of personal authority. With his self-directedness, he considers the world as a place of invention, a project in which he must creatively participate. As illustrated in Appendix A, personal initiative is reflected in the individual values of Stage III A—self-assertion, independence, empathy, generosity/service. With these values internalized, the individual can begin to actualize skills associated with Stage III B values—pioneerism/innovation/progress, construction/new order, accountability/mutual responsibility, mission/goals. While the Stage III A values tend to be interpersonal in nature, the Stage III B values reflect systems skills. Actually, the latter are the institutionalization of the former individual values. However, our observations have confirmed that Level 5 demands a jump in consciousness that brings to the person a clearer awareness of "system." The leader does not learn system skills and thus move into Level 5. Rather, he or she becomes aware that Level 5 is possible and then learns the system skills to realize it. Here we turn our attention to the conditions that facilitate the breaking-into-consciousness of this system awareness.

The Genesis of Systems Skills. As we examined the development of skills, we discovered a fascinating parallel between the historical development of mankind and the pattern of human growth in an individual. Man made a giant leap the moment he discovered the first tool. It was a hand tool—a hammer—a simple extension of his arm. This first tool, dated about two million years ago, marked the genesis of instrumental skills. Basically, instrumental skills make use of tools that in some way extend the body or the brain—as the crane extends the arm; the telescope, the eye; the computer, the brain itself.

Interestingly, in our work with executive leadership, we have found that professional competence increases as persons are more in touch with their bodies. Instrumentality is still an extension of the body! Thus, dieting, physical exercise, fasting and relaxation, and even meditation are helpful to the development of leaders, especially at higher levels. The evidence suggests that the body is primary to instrumentality. When the body is in tune—and in tune with the self—the person's instrumental skills will operate more effectively. We shall return to this concept of body-brain integration that enhances both instrumental and imaginal skills.

The second great event in the history of mankind produced a social invention and marked the beginning of civilization. Bronowski (1973, p. 60) believes that

> it is extraordinary to think that only in the last twelve thousand years has civilization, as we know it, taken off. There must have been an extraordinary explosion about 10,000 B.C.—and there was. But it was a quiet explosion. It was the end of the Ice Age.

The earth began to flower and men, who had been nomadic, suddenly stopped, stood still and began to tend the land. They became the Lords of the Earth; family life was born; the need to belong, then to be intimate, stirred in the human heart. Of the most powerful social revolution man has ever known, Bronowski continues,

> we have an anthopological record of the struggle of conscience of a people who made this decision: The record

is the Bible, the Old Testament. I believe civilization rests on the decision.

Again, we have noted in our work that the quality of a leader's relationships with the several groups of which he is a member is essential to leader-effectiveness. All interpersonal skills have their genesis in family life but affect the quality of all group life.

We digress briefly from our discussion of the genesis of systems skills to make some observations that grow out of our consultation experience and from our study of skill development. We pick up the concept of body-brain integration mentioned above and to it we add the necessity of an integrated group life. It has been our experience that to maintain high-level interpersonal skills and to acquire an effective systems awareness, the individual leader must have four aspects of his life intact. We have come to refer to these aspects as the four integrations.

The first of the four integrations we call **knowledge integration.** By this we mean that the leader's technical competence, that is his cognitive and imaginal skills, is so well developed that he can personally manage and make sense out of crisis situations. "Meaning-making" and the capacity to make intellectual sense out of seemingly disparate data without becoming overanxious assume the kind of "body-brain" integration we described above. It is the integration of minimal skills from the first four levels of leadership: skills of risk and survival; skills of rote and continual learning; skills of management administration; and the skill of an integrative imagination. The person who possesses this kind of knowledge integration is able to synthesize complex data from emotional as well as informational sources.

The other three integrations concern the leader's group life. **Family** or **intimacy integration** exists when the leader enjoys a sound "support system" at home. Normally, this is the family. It is our contention that at this level the leader's personal intimacy needs must be met. The leader must also experience a good work-group relationship—what we call **management team integration.** Although he may still be "boss," his work group interacts as adults. The "give-and-take" of good adult interaction does not happen accidentally; the leader possesses the skill to create and maintain a well-functioning team. Finally, the leader enjoys a **professional peer integration** that we described in our section on laissez-

* Note: The above four integrations occur in an adapted form in **The Report of the Lambeth Conference 1978** (CIO Publishing, London 1978, p. 79) where Hall was consultant to the Archbishop of Canterbury.

faire leadership. When this occurs, the leader experiences a solid peer group support in which he or she can share with other leaders at the same level problems in any of the categories above. It is assumed that the members of the family group, the work group, and the peer group are all different individuals.

It has been our experience that when an executive experiences a breakdown in more than one of these four integrations or if the groups are not mutually exclusive, he or she will begin to deteriorate within a twelve-month period. That is to say, one of three consequences is likely to occur. The leader will regress to an earlier form of leadership style; he will become disabled physically; or he will suffer severe emotional distress. Put in a more positive light, if the individual possesses the intellectual capacity and if his family meets his needs for personal intimacy, then the institution can do much to insure the remaining two integrations. The leader at Level 5 recognizes the need and will struggle to realize these four aspects of an integrated leadership life-cycle. Our experience leads us to believe that it is out of these conditions that the "jump in consciousness" occurs which brings the person to a clearer awareness of "system." It is then that system skills can be fully developed.

When we recall the sequency of skill development, we observe that technical or instrumental skills are the primary concerns of leadership Levels 1 and 2. Levels 3 and 4 are characterized by the emergence of interpersonal skills. With the vision of a Phase Three consciousness, the self assumes an ascendancy that puts personal creativity with its accompanying imaginal skills into a new prominence—Levels 4 and 5. Finally, if his total life-experience is integrated, a systems awareness breaks into consciousness at Level 5 enabling the initial development of systems skills. Figure 3.5 relates the emergence

EMERGENCE OF SKILLS	LEVELS OF LEADERSHIP			
Instrumental Skills	1 2			
Interpersonal Skills		3 4		
New Imaginal Skills			4 5	
Systems Skills				5 6
PHASE OF CONSCIOUSNESS	**ONE**	**TWO**	**THREE**	**FOUR**

Figure 3.5:—The emergence of skills in relationship to the levels of leadership and the phases of consciousness.

of skills to the levels of leadership and the phase of consciousness.

Systems skills depend upon the integration of instrumental and interpersonal skills developed during the first two phases of consciousness with the new imaginal skills that accompany the emergence of self at Phase Three. Although imaginal skills—wonder, discovery, and self-delight—arise during infancy, imagination and creativity become owned as distinct, unique gifts during Phase Three. Since fantasy and feeling are interrelated, the Phase Three person experiences the freedom to be unintimidated by sexual fantasy, to allow his anger to rise as a positive force, to feel that his ideas are as important as anyone else's. He or she experiences the freedom to go public with visions and dreams. Systems skills arise only after the leader has grown past Level 4, after he has taken ownership of his own personal authority, after his imagination begins to free his interpersonal capacity, and his feeling life begins to enrich his fantasy. As illustrated in Figure 3.6,

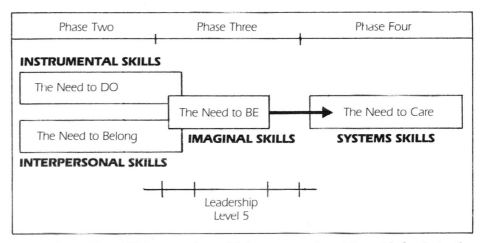

Figure 3.6:—The skill integration which occurs at Level 5 and is basic to the emergence of systems skills

the Phase Three need to **be** oneself transforms the earlier need to **do** and to **belong** and builds the bridge to a Phase Four vision. The freedom of the independent man is to no avail unless it is harnessed. If anger is not a tool for building the mutually accountable community, if imagination does not become corporate vision, then the self has become selfish. The freedom of the independent man is harnessed by the need to **care** that is expressed in those organizational communities which are both efficient and life enhancing. It is this kind of leadership that is desperately needed in society today.

Systems Skills: The Bridge to Level 6. Basically, systems skills depend upon an ability to see parts in relationship to the whole. To deal with a system means that the leader can differentiate interpersonal needs from system needs but synthesize them when necessary. System skills include the ability to use funds and financial systems as a means, to move comfortably with process, to clarify group complexity, to synthesize complex data, cognitive and emotional, to speak with clarity and to communicate with persons at different stages of development. These skills can develop in the leader whose total life experience is integrated—his skills, his family group, his work group, his peer group—and the independent man has become the creator man of Level 6.

Level 6 leadership is essentially different from previous levels in that it recognizes that leadership must be plural. Interdependence and harmony are the two values inherently necessary for such collegial authority. The leader is a facilitator of interdependent peer resources. The institutional values of Phase Three B—Appendix A—accountability/mutual responsibility, supportive community, construction/new order, even contemplation and presence have been internalized. The leader has sufficient skill with creative aggression to confront, even terminate, a person caringly. He or she can develop a peer support community not only to survive but to enhance the quality of life. The values of contemplation and health are taken seriously. The skill capacity to use diet, physical exercise, meditation, and relaxation techniques in order that the body-system function at its optimal level is seen as an integral part of daily life. The internalization of these values gives rise to the vision of Phase Four A values of interdependence, intimacy and solitude as unitive, truth/wisdom, and personal harmony.

The servant-leader role emerges with Level 6 provided that all four types of skills develop confluently. An individual at Phase Three with highly developed skills could be a con-artist or manipulator as easily as he could be a creative leader in society. Systems skills can be used against, rather than for society; they can be used for personal gain. Confluent skill development means that attention is paid to insure that all skills—instrumental, imaginal, interpersonal, and system—develop equally. In contrast, it is possible for an individual to develop the cognitive aspects of systems skills, but have very poorly developed interpersonal skills. As a consequence, destructive decisions occur—unconsciously. The system collapses or becomes inhuman.

The servant-leader is distinguished by the kinds of questions he raises institutionally. The Level 6 executive uses the concept of limited design criteria in planning for the organization. His central idea is to create a management design that maximizes the possible development of all individuals within the system,which guards the efficiency of the organization, and which tends to the good of society as a whole. The servant leader is interested not only in what is produced by the organization, but also in the quality of human interaction within the organization and the impact of the organization on the quality of life in society. The Phase Four vision of the world as mystery-to-be-cared-for underlies the activities of the servant leader as he or she seeks to give life to the global world.

Servant Leadership Summarized. Servant Leadership can be achieved by persons whose skills enable them to function comfortably within Phase Three consciousness and whose vision includes a Phase Four view of the world as mystery-to-be-cared-for. With the emergence of Phase Three consciousness, the individual experiences personal authority as unique; he values, in a new way, his personal creativity and imagination. The development of the new imaginal skills serves to integrate and enhance previously learned instrumental and interpersonal skills creating the bridge to the development of systems skills. It has been our experience that the four skill areas are integrated and develop confluently when the conditions in four areas of an individual's life are favorable. The leader's cognitive skill development is commensurate with the complexity of his position and responsibility and the degree of effectiveness of his or her work group, intimacy group, and peer group of mutually exclusive persons. The creator man, who shares the vision of the men of ideas—a Gandhi, an Illich, or a Shumacher whose values include those of Phase Four, and whose confluent skill development incarnates them in leadership behavior, is the servant leader so desperately needed in our times.

Chapter IV

Motivation: Why Some Persons Lead and Others, Who Could, Do Not

Based on Hall's theory of consciousness development with its associated values and skills, we have identified seven distinct styles of leadership that relate to the psychological maturity of both leaders and followers. Each style contributes to the development of leadership at a later level. We have examined the processes of growth that occur as an individual moves through the seven levels, and have described conditions that optimally facilitate the development of leaders in their journey toward servant leadership.

Our experience has made it even more clear that leaders develop within the context of institutions and that in reality, it

is impossible to separate leadership development from organizational renewal. We have come to realize that the leader is in a direct and symbiotic relationship with his or her institution. In fact, we believe that an institution is no more than the projection into reality of a leader's imagination. Our organizations are what we make of them!

At a time when the world so desperately needs servant leaders, self-initiating persons who will create, not merely maintain, we are haunted by the question of human motivation. What motivates some leaders to lead, and others, who could lead, to choose security? Robert Greenleaf (1977, p. 45) reflects on this problem:

> Too many (good and vital people) settle for being critics and experts. There is too much intellectual wheel spinning, too much retreating into "research," too little preparation and willingness to undertake the hard and high risk tasks of building better institutions in an imperfect world, too little disposition to see "the problem" as residing **in here** and not **out there. In short, the enemy is strong, natural servants who have the potential to lead but do not lead, or who choose to follow a non-servant**.

In this chapter we examine the problem of motivation within the consciousness-value theory and suggest possible ways in which individuals and institutions can consciously address the question of motivation. We conclude with two case studies followed by several observations synthesizing our experience in using the consciousness-value based approach in management consultation.

Toward A Theory of Motivation

The solution to the question, "what motivates this person to lead and that person to choose security?" may always remain a mystery. However, when we recall our earlier discussions of consciousness and value development, we think we can shed some light on why some persons make the leap from Level 3 to Level 5 leadership and others, who could, do not. Clearly, an individual's quest for personal meaning and his value priorities bear directly on the question of what motivates him.

The consciousness theory described in Chapter II suggests that persons construct a world view in which they seek meaning by satisfying those needs which the self sees as inherent to that world view. As Figure 2.1 above illustrates, the

Phase One person satisfies the physical needs basic to survival while the Phase Two person does things to succeed in and to belong to a significant social world. In Phase Three social needs are replaced by personal needs—for self-direction and being one's self. In Phase Four an individual's needs become communal. These general categories of need become more specific in what we call "values," which originate in one's consciousness but are expressed in behavior. Values are human motivators that give a person meaning and at the same time shape his life-style.

The values we associate with Phases One and Two bear a strong similarity to what Maslow calls D-cognition values—basic physical needs and belonging social-ego needs. Values at Phase Three and beyond resemble Maslow's B-cognition values—his self-actualizing needs. In terms of leadership development, the leap from Level 3 to Level 5 means that the individual is no longer motivated by Maslow's D-cognition but rather finds meaning in self-actualizing values. Gellerman (1963, p. 176) offers an explanation that we feel distinguishes values in the first three leadership styles—Phases One and Two—from values in Phase Three in terms of their power to motivate behavior.

It would seem that the kinds of motives which can be diminished when enough rewards are given are operating as "satisfier," to use Herzberg's term. That is, they press themselves insistently upon the individual when they don't receive enough gratification, but lapse into insignificance when they do. Hunger pangs, sleeplessness, and even monetary power can be appeased and have relatively little motivating power when they are appeased; their power is felt principally when they are not being satisfied. A satisfier affects the individual more by its absence than by its presence.

This observation suggests that when the basic needs of Phases One and Two are met, the motivating power of Phases One and Two values is seriously diminished. For leaders at Levels 1, 2, and 3, values are "satisfiers" and tend to motivate more by their absence and motivate less when they are minimally met. Too much security can lead to a decline in the desire to produce or grow.

The leader at Level 4, having become less satisfied with his world of achievement, belonging, and conformity to external authority, begins to envision the world as invention in which the individual assumes ownership of his personal authority. But he also experiences increased anxiety at the

84

prospect of accepting responsibility for his personal choices. Typically, the laissez-faire leader of Level 4 clarifies, facilitates, and listens endlessly, but he cannot create closure, he cannot make a choice based on personal authority. As alternatives increase, apprehension mounts.

However, anxiety functions in another way. Arthur Koestler (1967) suggests that although need satisfaction is basic to motivation, there is only one master motive—anxiety. He further explains that anxiety is not simply a reaction to the environment that is external to us, but it is also an internal drive to create.

> The organism functions not merely by responding to the environment but by asking questions. The main incentive to its exploratory activities are novelty, surprise, conflict and uncertainty. The exploration drive may combine with, or be instrument drives—sex, nutrition, anxiety. But in its purest form—in play, latent learning, unrewarded problem solving—"stimuli" and "responses" are undistinguishable parts of the same feedback loop along which excitation is running in a circle like a kitten chasing its tail. "The scientist," wrote Allport, "by the very nature of his commitment, creates more and more questions, never fewer."

> Indeed, the measure of our intellectual maturity, one philosopher suggests, is our capacity to feel less and less satisfied with our answers to better problems. (p.507)

Koestler's comments suggest that the self-actualization values of Phase Three, in contrast to "satisfiers" of Phases One and Two, are never really "met" or "fulfilled" and consequently they continue to motivate, they continue to provoke an internal anxiety to quest.

For leaders at Level 4, who envision themselves as becoming self-initiating persons and whose environment presents them with numerous complex alternatives, anxiety is fed by two sources—the leader's internal drive to create and in reaction to the external demands that he make decisions from many alternatives. Anxiety, then, is key to what happens to leaders at Level 4. If the individual can overcome this barrier by becoming able to cope with increased levels of apprehension, he moves forward rapidly. If he or she is unable to cope with increased anxiety, the person returns to the security of Phase Two and probably functions as a Level 2 leader.

In summary, our view of motivation consists of three points. First, with Koestler we agree that anxiety is the master motive, which at Phases One and Two seeks to satisfy Maslow's D-cognition values—basic physical needs and belonging and social ego needs. Self-preservation and security are the primary values of Phase One while self-worth, belonging, self-confidence/competence are the primary values of Phase Two. Leaders at Levels 1–3, who rely on authority outside themselves—rules, expectations, tradition—experience a sense of contingency of being out-of-control with the world. The anxiety caused by this sense of contingency motivates them to meet security needs, or "satisfiers," to use Herzberg's terms.

Secondly, we concur with Koestler that anxiety accompanies the internal drive to create, to initiate, to be one's self, values characteristic of Phase Three and similar to Maslow's self-actualizing needs. Unlike security needs, which when "satisfied" cease to motivate, self-actualizing needs are never "satisfied" and continue to motivate. To act on one's own authority causes anxiety that mounts as the alternatives from which to choose increase in number and complexity. As the Level 4 leader aspires to values of self-actualization and personal authority so does his apprehension increase.

Finally, we believe that for the Level 4 leader to make choices based on his envisioned values of self-direction and personal authority, he or she must be able to overcome the barrier of increased anxiety. If the person learns to cope with it, he or she makes a tremendous leap forward. If unable to cope, the person becomes paralyzed.

The key, then, is to discover what enables a person to surmount the anxiety barrier and move from Level 3 to Level 5. We suggest three ways in which individuals can learn to cope effectively with the increased anxiety inherent in Phase Three: (1) integrated skill development, (2) support groupings, and (3) opportunity within the organization.

Integrated Skill Development. For the leader at Level 4, it is essentail that the individual become aware of and begin to practice the new imaginal skills that are associated with self-actualization and personal authority so that these can become integrated with the well-developed instrumental and interpersonal skills associated with Phase Two. Figure 4.1, a modification of an earlier Figure (3.6) illustrating skill integration, schematically demonstrates the point in leadership development where consciously practiced imaginal skills begin to internalize the Phase Three value of self-actualization and raise existing instrumental and interpersonal skills to a new level.

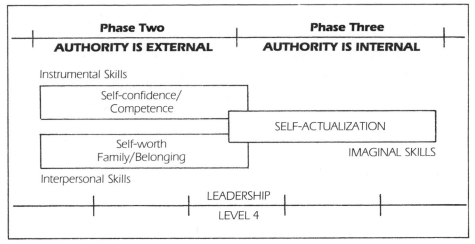

Figure 4.1:—The need for integrated skill development at Level 4 leadership style.

We recall from our discussion of imaginal skills in Chapter 1 (p. 30) that imagination is the synergetic interaction among the fantasy, the emotions, and the reflective intellect, all processes internal to the individual. While the imagination develops in early infancy, with the expansion of consciousness into a Phase Three vision, it takes on a whole new importance. The data received from one's inner world, the use of images to generate meaning, the evaluation of images by the emotions as helpful or harmful, and the construction of ideas are valued in themselves by individuals who accept their personal authority. Learning to trust one's inner self is awkward and takes practice. It requires delicate balance to avoid too much security on the one hand and too much apprehension on the other. Gellerman (1963, p. 178) observes that

> If the overhanging need can somehow be cleared away, the underlying one will increasingly take over and guide the individual into new interests and attitudes. He may seem like a "new" man, revealing unsuspected depths and potentialities. Yet he is not a new man at all; he is simply a more highly developed version of himself.

When the individual can separate him or herself from a need for continuous security, the imaginal skills develop and a new version of the person emerges as a Level 5 leader. When this happens, it can be said of the person that he possesses the knowledge integration we described in Chapter III, p. 77.

Support Groupings. For many persons, becoming aware of the nature of the new skills and expecting that their practice will feel awkward is helpful but not totally sufficient to carry them through the process. Often, it is not understood that the primary values of self-preservation, self-worth and self-confidence can reoccur in full force in every new situation. As a person enters the new world view of Phase Three, he or she will experience a new and frightening reoccurrence of insecurity, of inadequacy, and of low self-esteem. Furthermore, persons need the support of others when the choices they make based on new values do not work out well because the new values have not been internalized in personal action. An example and diagram can help illustrate the relationship between values as **vision, choice,** and **act** and the need for group support during the process of skill formation.

A Level 4 manager **envisions** improved employee-management relations within his division and wants to maintain full cooperation especially from Employee X. But Employee X, a line foreman, has been closing his eyes to a number of practices. It is the manager's **choice** to confront him and make the line foreman accountable. While the Level 4 manager is a good listener, his skill of empathy is not well developed. Consequently, when the manager goes to confront the line foreman who has been around for years, he cannot actually pull off his choice to confront. His **act** is not as well developed as his choice. He is in the process of forming the skill of empathy; it is not yet internalized. Figure 4.2 illustrates these relationships.

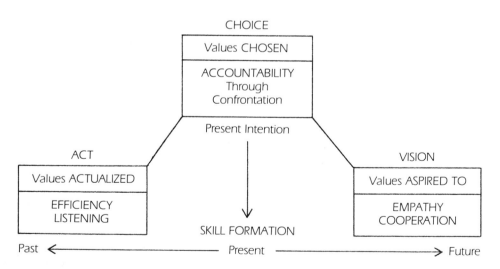

Figure 4.2:—Values as act, choice, and vision: The process of Skill Information.

The values of efficiency and listening, which have been actualized in the past, together with the manager's vision of empathy and cooperation within his division in the future form the dynamics of skill formation in the present. In the illustration, the manager's attempt to make the foreman accountable did not work. A bad experience can cause withdrawal if the reason for the failure is not understood. The manager needs to practice making people accountable, painful as the process may be. The development of his skills will enable him to accomplish the task, but an understanding support group will enable him to deal with the anxiety accompanying the process.

Although support can come from three separate groups—his work group, his family group, and a peer group—it is the peer group that must be initiated by the organization. If the organization does not encourage, even provide opportunities for its management personnel to create professional peer groups, it will often find executives forming friendships with inappropriate persons in the system. Such friendships frequently lead to difficult and unnecessary problems. Our experience has convinced us that a professional peer support structure is an essential ingredient to humanistic leader development. Without peer support structures being built into organizations, we are simply inviting rigid persons with insufficient interpersonal skills to be placed in positions of leadership.

Opportunity Within the Organization. To recognize the need for and to develop professional peer support structures is only one way organizations can provide opportunities for leader development. We agree with Stogdill (1974, p. 127) that "the trend toward minimizing the importance of personality and motivation in role mobility and in experiencing personal satisfaction has, perhaps, gone too far." Individuals are less motivated to grow when institutions fail to provide opportunities for growth.

We believe that opportunities for growth can be structured into the organization. Moreover, organizational leaders themselves can become sufficiently skilled in the value approach to use it effectively to the benefit both of individuals and institution itself. Leadership teams can develop skill in value-based goal setting and skill analysis. By so doing, they can be more in touch with the relationship between institutional values and goals and how these relate to the personal values of individuals within the institution. Staff development personnel can be trained to align an individual's value stance and skill needs to the needs of the institution in mutually beneficial ways. To accomplish this goal, they need to be able to identify the values of individuals and to place persons so as to reinforce positively the development of these values. They need to be able to challenge a person to the next

Level by creating individualized programs for leadership development. The two case studies that follow illustrate how organizations can provide opportunities for growth, mutually beneficial to the individual and the institution.

TWO CASE STUDIES

The Case of Joe. For ten years, Joe has been an administrator in a large community research agency. He holds degrees in social work and in business administration. Now, at age 55, he requests a change in position. He is interested in creating and then directing a staff-development program. As he envisioned it, he would continue with his responsibilities pertaining to the administration of the agency including documentation and the use of library resources. He would like to take on the orientation of new personnel and initiate some group-development activities with selected personnel so as to bring about new levels of cooperation within the agency and between agency personnel and the Board.

Joe discussed these ideas with the agency's director. During the course of the conversation it became fairly clear that some of Joe's values were institutional for which he had well-developed skills—administrative control, loyalty to the agency, prestige. Personal initiative values were beginning to emerge since he sought an outlet for creativity and self-direction. He asked to design a program and to test it out with selected staff. Joe and the director concluded that he could continue his present administrative responsibilities and that he possessed the capability for orienting new personnel, teaching them the agency's standard administration and documentation methods. These decisions reinforced Joe's present level of leadership.

In order for Joe to begin exercising his aspired-to-values, a schedule was set up that allowed him to direct three goups, two of which were to be on his own time. The schedule did not interfere with his administrative responsibilities and it was agreed that the agency's director would attend each group. It was not long before Joe became painfully aware that he lacked skill in encouraging group participation. One day he admitted, "I certainly could never run these group development sessions without regular personnel also being present!"

Four staff members, including the director, who had been group participants reflected with Joe concerning what was happening during the group sessions. They identified one incident that was particularly significant. Joe had been confronted by a young social worker who accused him of being too dictatorial and not open to the opinions of others. Joe talked with the group about his concerns during this incident and together they identified five values implicit in Joe's behavior—duty/obligation, loyalty/respect, on the one hand; empathy, sharing/listening/trust, and self-direction, on the other. When placed on a consciousness track, (Figure 4.3), they confirmed a notion that initially emerged during his conversation with the director, namely, that Joe was going through that awkward transition period between Phases Two and Three. His Stage III A values were those to which he aspired; he needed to think about the skills that would enable him to internalize them in his behavior.

PHASE TWO		PHASE THREE	
	Stage II B	Stage III A	
	Duty/Obligation Loyalty/Respect	Empathy Self-direction Sharing/Listening Trust	
		Level 4	

Figure 4.3:—Values plotted on consciousness track.

Since the values were interpersonal, the group talked about what might be included in interpersonal skills and then dialogued about the value "empathy," listing all the skills that might relate to it. When they followed the same procedure for the other Stage III A values, they noticed that many skills overlapped. From the final list of some fifty skills, it was easy to identify those skills Joe had already developed and to give priority to five he needed to develop to accomplish his goal. His final list included the following:

1. To identify one's own feelings accurately;
2. To identify the feelings of others;
3. To state anger objectively;
4. To differentiate between an interpersonal conflict and a group problem;
5. To enable a group to resolve its problem as a group and avoid becoming involved in personal conflict.

As a consequence of this session, Joe agreed to take a human-relations workshop extending over three weekend periods at a local college. Within the next two years, Joe's skills developed sufficiently for him to move into a full-time position divided equally between staff development and supervision of administrators. Joe worked at developing the skills that enabled him to make the transition to Phase Three; the organization provided the opportunity; and his administrative team supported him during a period of increased anxiety.

The Case of Mr. Patel. Mr. Patel is the executive vice president and part owner of a multinational engineering and export business. Located in the Middle East, the company makes air-conditioning and refrigeration parts. Of the fifteen hundred employees, one-third are unskilled labor.

Mr. Patel described his problem as difficulty in managing time. It was his responsibility to work out the long-term financing and general development of two new overseas operations. But he felt that he spent too much time coordinating the three division heads responsible to him—marketing, accounting, and production. He lamented that long hours at work kept him from his family and his physical condition was degenerating. Finally he said, "The three men in charge of marketing, accounting, and production do not coordinate themselves. When I delegate the responsibility, it just does not happen!"

The consultant (in this case the company had called in external consultation) listened to a number of conflict situations that Mr. Patel felt were significant to him. Through the conversation, the values he chose to live by could be identified. These included human dignity, empathy, self-actualization, cooperation, accountability/mutual responsibility. Mr. Patel's values indicated a Level 5 leadership style.

The consultant then inquired about the four integrations. He found Mr. Patel ranked high on three Integrations. He was intelligent; he enjoyed an intimate family life; he had a sound professional peer group in the members of a local club who met once a month. But when it came to work group cooperation, it simply did not exist.

Subsequently there were several meetings with the three divisional heads. Strangely, Mr. Patel whose values indicated Level 5 leadership style was experienced by the others as a benevolent dictator—a Level 2 leader! He listened but could not delegate; he cared, but as a father to his sons. Later, when the matter of delegating the role of coordinator to one of the three divisional heads was suggested, they all remained silent. After the meeting, one of the divisional heads confided that

Mr. Patel often talked about delegation, but that he never took him seriously because he was sure that in the near future Mr. Patel's son would be put into the position of coordinator.

In a conversation with Mr. Patel and the company president, several cultural factors were identified that shed light on the situation. In the Middle East, patriarchal authority has always been assumed. Marriage is arranged by parents; the son follows the father. When transferred into the business world, these attitudes expect the organizational structure to be bureaucratic and leadership to rest in one person.

It was not the consultant's intention to impose a new way of life on this company, yet it was hoped that the company's executive level leadership would understand the value conflict they were experiencing. What values did Mr. Patel want to enact? What did he mean by human dignity and cooperation? In response, Mr. Patel made three significant observations. (1) "My son is going to be a surgeon and will not join the business." (2) "If we do achieve 'team' management, even though I remain the boss, we will not only operate more efficiently, but I will be able to spend more time at home." (3) "I would like to see these three men grow in the business, but they refuse." When asked if he had shared these thoughts with his divisional heads, he replied, "No. I did not know how without appearing to be incompetent."

The next day the consultant talked with the divisional heads in an effort to determine their value level and the value level of those immediately below them. The divisional heads emphasized efficiency, productivity, administration/control and competence. These are Phase Two values; the divisional heads were organization men—Level 3. It was their job to remain loyal to the organization. A further analysis suggested that most of the personnel supervised by the divisional heads valued most their security—Phase One—and viewed the managers as paternal leaders. Again, the cultural pattern reinforced this followership style. Each of the divisional heads had well-developed instrumental skills; each knew the work of his division well. Only one, the marketing head, also understood production and accounting. He showed some values and skills concerned with cooperation and sharing/listening/trust. The next task for the consultant was to share with Mr. Patel and the divisional heads what he felt was happening. It appeared that Mr. Patel envisioned team cooperation; he chose to delegate responsibility, but in actual fact the delegated responsibility was not accepted, and Mr. Patel himself coordinated. Schematically, Mr. Patel's problem is illustrated in Figure 4.3 below.

Mr. Patel's time-management problem was not exclusively his own but involved each of the divisional heads. The consultant began the final stage of enabling the group of four persons to understand what was happening. A set of strategies was developed with the group, allowing it to become a corporate team and at the same time respecting the vision and skill level of each of the members.

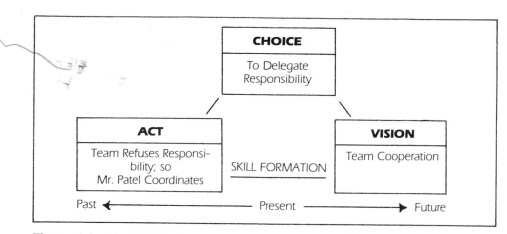

Figure 4.3—Mr. Patel's time-management problem as act-choice-vision

During the next two years the following events occurred. First, an external coordinator was hired, a mature man who had recently retired from an executive position. He coordinated the team on Mr. Patel's behalf by meeting weekly with the entire group. Secondly, Mr. D'Souza, the marketing manager, was given training in group dynamics and team building. Thus, he was "coached" into the position of coordinator. By the second year, Mr. D'Souza took over the responsibilities of coordinator in addition to his own work as marketing manager. Finally, this team began to explore ways to set up a training division to insure that future leadership could come from company personnel. Organizational charts demonstrate the transition from Mr. Patel's original situation to the arrangements that existed when the team itself functioned in a coordinated way. Figures 4.4 to 4.6 illustrate the three stages.

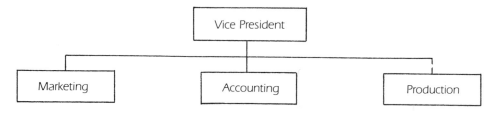

Figure 4.4:—Year one: Mr. Patel coordinates.

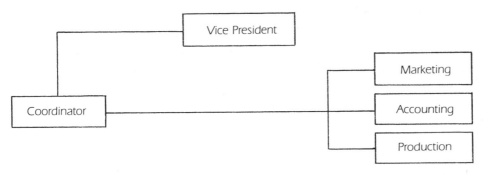

Figure 4.5:—Year two: An external coordinator builds an administrative team.

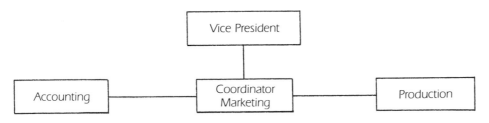

Figure 4.6:—Year three: The divisional head of marketing coordinates the administrative team.

The arrangements realized in the third year retain Mr. Patel in his position of authority; his vision of an administrative team has been actualized; Mr. D'Souza has developed skills that internalize values that began to emerge during year one. The other two divisional heads are experiencing what a team-administrative approach might mean for them personally, a new vision

Some Final Observations

The example of Mr. Patel, supported by our experience with executives from over twenty-five countries, leads us to believe that a value analysis of leadership styles may well be a potent instrument for developing holistic and socially creative leaders on an international level. Value analysis, done carefully, enlightens; it does not impose a foreign set of values on individuals or organizations. It continues to amaze us that the consensus for what the standard of leadership "should be," regardless of nationality, religion, or politics, is the Level 6 standard of human dignity and societal renewal. Social reconstruction, based on this approach, is a process of conscientization and the technical ability to make operational the values of which one becomes conscious.

Based on our experience with corporate executives, religious leaders, and agency administrators from various cultural backgrounds, we have become aware of several outcomes resulting from a value-analysis approach to leadership. We share these for their potential value. When value-based methods are used consistently to develop organizational goals and objectives, several outcomes occur:

1. A strong bond is built among personnel who have become conscientized to the value that they and the company hold in common.

2. Organizational leaders become more fully aware of the harmony or disharmony that exists between the organization's values and the values of the society or the local community.

3. Motivation toward realizing the corporate policies is significantly increased when the personnel concerned become aware of a common set of value priorities.

4. Problem-solving in the area of interpersonal conflict is often simplified and made more objective when there is a consensus on the "expected norms" for the organization that rests on value-based goals.

When the value-based approach is used to analyze an entire organization and its administrative personnel for the purpose of developing the skills of executives and other managers, several interesting outcomes occur.

1. Individualized leadership-development programs, designed specifically for the person, can also be directed toward the achievement of a corporate objective. In other words, personal skill development enables an executvie to internalize, through the skill developed, one of the company's values.

2. Corporate loyalty increases as common skill-building begins to actualize organizational values.

3. Individual evaluation is more holistic when comprehensive skill inventories have been developed for all management personnel.

4. Hiring and promotion practices are significantly improved when personnel managers approach these decisions with a background in assessing maturity level in terms of consciousness, values, and skill development.

5. The local community benefits when an organization's entire work-force begins to experience in their leader's growth toward Levels 5 and 6.

6. A natural evaluation process occurs if a value and skill analysis occurs every two years.

7. Skill development based on a value analysis helps eliminate conflicts that tend to grow out of cross-cultural

ituations. Common corporate values can provide a work base even when cultural values may be in conflict.

8. Problems in communication between persons in one phase of consciousness and those in another phase can be reduced when the person in a later phase learns to speak a language that is meaningful to persons in an earlier phase. Executives in Third World nations as well as labor-relations personnel in our own country frequently encounter problems where the conflict is actually a difference in phase of consciousness.

9. The healthy growth of all employees of the company, indeed of the local community, can result when general training programs within the organization select skills for development from each of the four skill areas—instrumental, interpersonal, imaginal, and system.

Leadership Theory Revisited

As an epilogue to our discussion on a value approach to the development of leadership, we return to our opening chapter that surveyed leadership theory. How do the Levels of leadership and the consciousness-value framework that supports them relate to current administrative theory and leadership-training practice? We share our conclusions by focusing on three points. We believe that Hall's levels of leadership are grounded in current administrative theory; that the consciousness-value-skill development approach builds on but goes beyond present theory and practice; and finally, that our journey toward servant leadership raises questions about how we can better prepare the leaders of our future.

Leadership Levels and Administrative Theory and Research. In reviewing the survey of administrative theory, we asked several questions. At what level would a manager who followed McGregory's theory X be operating? theory Y? In terms of leadership level, what values are emphasized by the

"team" style "9,9" on Blake and Mouton's managerial grid? How do the levels of leadership account for the distinctions made by Katz and Kahn: administration, interpolation, and origination? Does sensitivity training fit into the model? We raised these questions in an imaginative way, hoping to see new relationships rather than to categorize and limit.

We suggest that the alienated man, as a Level 1 leader, is the manager who follows McGregor's theory X. His style is autocratic: he assumes that workers are indolent, dependent, and usually unintelligent; he cares only about getting the job done. While a Level 2 leader probably envisions theory Y, it seems that the organization man, who has well developed instrumental and interpersonal skills, internalizes theory Y assumptions in his administrative behavior. As a person firmly within Phase Two consciousness, he values both achievement and acceptance, productivity and personal concern. When we reflected on the managerial grid, a similar relationship suggested itself. Blake and Mouton's "ask manager," "9" in his concern for production, "1" in his concern for people, describes Level 1 leadership. The "team manager," "9" on both his concern for production and for people, describes the Phase Two individual who is both efficient and personable, our Level 3 organization man.

When we reflected on the remaining quadrants of the managerial grid, an interesting question arose. Is there not a resemblance between the Level 4, laissez-faire leader, and the "1,9" quadrant where the "club leader" exhibits great concern for people but little gets done? He listens endlessly, but decisions are never made. It also seems that human-relations programs, particularly sensitivity training, might relate to Level 4 leadership that we see only as a short-lived transition from Level 3 to Level 5. Sensitivity training in itself does not make the democratic leader of Level 5, but it may enable a person, whose education and experience have emphasized the development of instrumental skills, to enter more fully and value the inner world of human emotion, his own and others.

Finally, when we looked at the distinctions Katz and Kahn have made, we feel that the "influential increment" that distinguishes administration and interpolation from origination bears a strong resemblance to the differences between Level 3 and Levels 5 and 6. Here the leadership style relates less to the behavior chosen by the individual and more to the nature of the task demanded by the level of leadership within the organization's hierarchy. The nature of the task for a college registrar demands that he or she have technical knowledge and an understanding of how the systems operate. These are the instrumental skills required by "administration," as Katz and Kahn describe it. In contrast, the task of a college president expects that the individual will possess an "intellective aspect of leadership" characteristic of origination. We believe the "intellective aspect" can be equated with the new imaginal skills that develop with Phase Three and the development of systems skills that follow. We would expect a college registrar to function in a style characteristic of Level 3; a college president, at Level 5 or 6. Figure 5.1 suggests how these several administrative theories relate to the levels of leadership.

PHASE OF CONSCIOUSNESS and LEVEL OF LEADERSHIP Related to ADMINISTRATIVE THEORIES	Phase One		Phase Two		Phase Three		Phase Four
	1	2	3	4	5	6	7
McGregor Theory X Theory Y							
Blake and Mouton Task 9,1 Team 9,9 Club 1,9							
Katz and Kahn Administration Interpolation Origination							

Figure 5.1:—Possible relationships between levels of leadership and administrative theories.

Since our experience has convinced us that leadership styles can never be separated from followership style because both are directly related to the maturity of the leader and of the led, we are particularly interested in playing with possible relationships between the levels of leadership and the ideas of Sweney and Fiechtner as well as the "life-cycle theory" of Hersey and Blanchard. Sweney and Fiechtner suggest that organizations are sustained by diametrically opposed behavior on the part of those in superordinate and subordinate roles. The authoritarian leader who retains power needs the ingratiating follower who respects power. The laissez-faire leader who denies power to himself needs the rebel who seeks power for himself. The egalitarian leader who shares power needs cooperators with whom to share power. These three dominant leader-follower roles bear a strong resemblance to at least five of the Levels of leadership. Figure 5.2 can be compared with Figure 3.4 or Appendix C for an extended description of the styles. It is interesting to note that the role-confusion between leader and follower at Level 4 does not seem similar to Sweney and Fiechtner's permissive leader who needs a rebel to seek the power he denies to himself. It does seem significant that Sweney and Fiechtner suggest that a **sustaining** relationship is achieved by these diametrically opposed behavior patterns. In our experience the role confusion of Level 4 cannot be sustained and the leadership style is short-lived. One might say that the rebel who successfully seeks power for himself becomes the new automcratic leader even though he may not actually hold a position of leadership.

Level 1	Level 2	Level 3	Level 4	Level 5	Level 6
AUTOCRATIC LEADERS as Dictators Godfathers Bureaucrats			LAISSEZ-FAIRE LEADERS	DEMOCRATIC LEADERS as Charismatic Collegial Creators Servants	
who RETAIN POWER need — — ↓↑ — — — INGRATIATING FOLLOWERS who RESPECT POWER			REBEL FOLLOWERS	who SHARE POWER need — — ↓↑ — — COOPERATING FOLLOWERS who can accept SHARED POWER	

Figure 5.2:—Some relationships between three dominant leader-follower roles of Sweney and Fiechtner and the Levels of leadership.

In addition to this symbiotic relationship between leader and followers, Sweney and Fiechtner suggest that these three dominant roles follow a pattern of maturation, a pattern implicit in the levels of leadership. Hersey and Blanchard's "life-cycle theory" also supports the notion that "psychological maturity" determines appropriate leader behavior. "Psychological maturity" can be estimated by the individual's ability to set goals, to take responsibility for his own performance, and his level of education and experience. When we combine the second situational dimension, the nature of the task, to the psychological maturity of the group, and then ask about appropriate leader behavior within the consciousness-value framework, some interesting possibilities emerge. Again, we revisit the managerial grid giving special attention to the "club" and "apathetic" styles of leadership. In Figure 1.2 we superimposed the four quadrants of the life-cycle theory on the managerial grid suggesting that leadership in a law firm might indeed demand "club" style leadership. In those rather rare institutions such as think tanks, apparent "apathy" might be the most appropriate management style. It is interesting to speculate about the implications of tentatively identifying the "life cycle-quadrants" with the four phases of consciousness as illustrated in Figure 5.3.

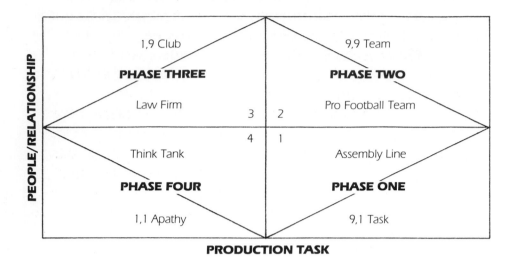

Figure 5.3:—The managerial grid, "life-cycle quadrants", and the phases of consciousness: Are these related?

Finally, the notion of Katz and Kahn that leadership processes differ—administration, interpolation, origination—bears a similarity to the skills emphasized at the five Levels of leadership illustrated in the matrix presented in Figure 1.3. Based on the work of Clement, Ayres, and Zierdt, this matrix of organization leadership identifies nine types of skills associated with five organization leader levels. They claim that these skills undergo a character change as the person employing them moves up the organizational hierarchy. For example, planning might include scheduling at a lower level while at a higher level it might involve an environmental-impact study. The lower-level positions tend to emphasize instrumental and interpersonal skills—technical competence, supervision, communication, and human relations—which can only become fully developed with the emergence of a Phase Three consciousness. If there is validity to this idea, then we can expect that as leader positions move from lower to higher levels within an organization, the nature of the leadership task will change in a pattern similar to the levels of leadership styles. We might expect a first-line supervisor to function at least at Level 2; low-level and middle managers might be expected to operate at Levels 3 or 4; executives and policy-makers, at Levels 5 or 6.

From these comparisons, it seems fair to conclude that the levels of leadership based on Hall's theory of consciousness and values are consistent with current

102

administrative theory and research. We recognize that some relationships are stronger than others; some similarities are grounded in the same theory and research. We also acknowledge that in some areas we fancifully speculate with the hope of ultimately discovering new insights.

An Effort to Build On but Go Beyond. While Hall's levels of leadership theory builds on our current understanding of leadership, its framework in the development of consciousness and values goes well beyond the present state of administrative art. The consciousness-value theory provides structure that supports a holistic approach to human growth. By identifying phases in the development of consciousness and their associated values, we can better understand differences among large, and very distinct, groups of people as well as differences within the development of individuals. When these differences in meaning and value systems are understood, persons at later phases of consciousness can learn to communicate with and be heard by persons at earlier phases. Since the phases are developmental in nature, persons who choose to grow can be enabled to acquire skills that internalize their envisioned values. Caring persons can enable leadership to develop. Since the levels of followership are also developmental, caring persons can seek to create for others good experiences of leadership at each level. When followers have good experiences of leadership at lower levels, they build the base that enables them to become leaders at the higher levels. For affluent Americans whose lives may have been spared the pain of a hostile Phase One world, this may mean experiencing the rigors of survival in structured programs such as Outward Bound. Finally, we feel that the vision provided by the prophets of Phase Four can enable some persons to choose the path toward servant leadership while others can choose to follow only leaders who are also servants.

Appendix A: Ends Values in Their Stage of Development

| | Phase One | | Phase Two | | Phase Three | | Phase Four | |
	Stage I A	Stage I B	Stage II A	Stage II B	Stage III A	Stage III B	Stage IV A	Stage IV B
PRIMARY or CORE VALUES	Self-preservation	Security	Self-worth/ Family/ Belonging	Self-confidence/ Competence	Life/Self-actualization Service/ Vocation	Being Self Human Dignity	Intimacy/ Solitude	Ecority/ Beauty Transcendence/Global Confluence
OTHER ENDS VALUES	Self-centeredness Wonder/ Awe/ Fate	Self-delight	Self-control Fantasy/ Play	Work/Labor Play/ Leisure	Equality/ Liberation Integration/ Wholeness	Art/Beauty Construction/ New Order Contemplation/ Asceticism Education/ Knowledge/ Insight Knowledge/ Discovery/ Insight Presence/ Dwelling Ritual/ Meaning	Harmony-Personal Truth/ Wisdom/ Intuitive insight	Harmony-System

Means Values in Their Stage of Development

	Stage I A	Stage I B	Stage II A	Stage II B	Stage III A	Stage III B	Stage IV A	Stage IV B
PRIME SKILL VALUES	Safety/Survival		Instrumentality / Family/Belonging	Education/Certification	Empathy Health Independence	Accountability/Mutual Responsibility	Interdependence	Convivial Tools Intermediate Technology
OTHER MEANS VALUES	Food/Warmth/Shelter	Affection/Physical Discovery/Delight Economics/Profit Property/Control Sensory Pleasure/Sex Wonder/Curiosity	Being Liked Courtesy/Respect Equilibrium Friendship/Belonging Function Obedience/Duty Prestige/Image Social Affirmation Support/Peer Tradition	Achievement/Success Administration/Control Communications Competition Control/Order/Discipline Criteria/Rationality Duty/Obligation Economics/Success Efficiency Honor Instrumentality Law/Rule Loyalty/Respect Management Membership/Institution Objectivity Ownership Patriotism/Esteem Productivity Responsibility Rule/Accountability Workmanship/Craft	Adaptability/Flexibility Self-assertion Congruence Self-directedness Equity/Rights Evaluation/Self System Expressiveness/Freedom Generosity/Service Law/Guide Limitation/Celebration Obedience/Mutual Accountability Power/Authority Honesty Relaxation Search/Meaning Sharing/Listening/Trust	Community-Supportive Cooperation Corporation/Construction/New Order Creativity/Ideation Detachment/Solitude Growth/Expansion Intimacy Justice Missions/Goals Pioneerism/Innovation/Progress Pluiformity Recreation/Freesence Research/Originality/Knowledge Simplicity/Play	Community-Personalist Synergy Word	Macro Economics

105

Appendix B. Values as Skills

	Stage I A	Stage I B	Stage II A	Stage II B	Stage III A	Stage III B	Stage IV A	Stage IV B
IMAGINAL SKILLS	Wonder/Awe/Fate	Self-delight	Play/Fantasy			Art/Beauty		Ecority/Beauty
		Discovery/Delight/Wonder/Curiosity				Creativity/Ideation		
INSTRUMENTAL SKILLS				Self-competence/Confidence Work/Labor		Education/Knowledge/Insight Knowledge/Discovery/Insight		
	Food/Warmth/Shelter/Safety/Survival	Economics/Profit Property/Control	Function	Achievement/Success Administration/Control Communications Competition Control/Order Discipline Criteria/Rationality Economics/Success Education/Certification Efficiency Institution/Membership Instrumentality Law/Rule Management Objectivity Productivity Rule/Accountability Workmanship/Craft		Pioneerism/Innovation/Progress Research/Originality Knowledge Simplicity/Play		